Forged
in the Fire

Shaped by the Master

Forged
in the Fire

Shaped by the Master

Tim Burns

HENSLEY
PUBLISHING
6116 E. 32nd St.
Tulsa, OK 74135

ISBN 1-56322-086-5

Forged in the Fire — Shaped by the Master

About Photocopying This Book

Contents

Introduction

When gold ore is first mined from the ground, the precious metal is mixed with many impurities. In its natural, unconverted state, gold is not the precious and beautiful substance that we normally think of — instead it is a dark, cloudy mixture of gold, tin, and other common metals the Old Testament writers called "dross." Only placing the gold in a ceramic cup and holding it over a blazing furnace would cause the gold to separate from the dross. At high temperatures, the impurities would float to the top and were poured off, leaving that which the master sought: pure gold of highest value.

In the same way, our loving Father desires to temper our hearts and purge the imperfections in our character. Charles Spurgeon put it this way:

> It is because He loves us so much that He tries us by delaying His answers of peace…. Love closes the hand of divine bounty and restrains the outflow of favor when it sees that a solid gain will ensue from a period of trial…. Who would desire to see the gold taken out of the fire before its waste is consumed? Wait, O precious thing, until you have gained the utmost of purity! These furnace moments when you are in the hands of God, are profitable. It would be unwise to shorten such golden hours. The time of the promise corresponds with the time most enriching to the heart and soul.[1]

The four people we will consider in this Bible study were each a distinctive leader of the Israelite nation: King David; Joseph, the Israelite prince of Egypt; and Kings Saul and Hezekiah. Each of these great men led God's people through different events in their nation's history. Two of them are acclaimed for their examples, which inspire us to this day. The other two allowed their hearts to be swept away from God by the everyday cares of life. Their flaws foreshadowed their eventual downfall. What were the differences between the lives of these men? What made them become the men that they were? And more importantly, in what ways can you become a person through whom God can work? These are the questions we will investigate in this Bible study.

As you work your way through this book, you will consider each principle as it is unearthed and then ask yourself the difficult question, "What about me?" Each week you will have the opportunity to delve into God's Word, experience the text "brought to life" in narrative form, and begin to apply the principles from the passage to your own life. You will begin to ask, in comparison to the men that are studied, how do you allow God to work in your own life? Give God free reign to work in your spirit throughout this study, so that what was said of David will also become true of you, that you will become a man or woman "after God's own heart." As you examine the principles to building godly character that are outlined within these pages, it is my prayer that you will discover that God is closer and more active in your life than you ever realized. He is willing to work with your insecurities and imperfections. At the same time, He calls you to ascend the steps of His temple, look into His face, and find the courage to make the decision to become more like Him.

This Bible study will take you through God's process of converting your selfish, sinful nature into a reflection of God's glory. If you are a new Christian who is growing in your faith, you will find strength and courage to reach new heights in your walk with God. If you are a Christian who feels stuck in the events life has thrown into your path, you will find encouragement to know that God is walking the path with you. If you are a person struggling just to know who God is and how He wants to be a part of your life, these pages can bring you a deeper understanding of the unfathomable love and the limitless compassion that God has for you. Blessings as you begin your personal journey to be *Forged in the Fire — Shaped by the Master.*

SECTION ONE
David

Introduction to Section One

Of all the men and women in the Bible, the shepherd who rose to Israel's throne is one of the most colorful, diverse, and well-known characters. The youngest son in a large family, David carried the typical stigma of being the "family runt." He was left on his own to herd sheep, and his older brothers didn't want much to do with their ruddy, pipsqueak little brother. Yet, this same boy grew into the man who defended his father's sheep from lions and bears. When he killed a Philistine giant with a single stone from his slingshot, he became a national hero and was promoted to the captain of the military. But despite his courage and bravado, David had a sensitive side and wrote poetry — including much of the book of Psalms. His songs soothed the habitually despondent King Saul, but David still led victorious military campaigns that won him national recognition.

Despite all of the acclaim he garnered in his lifetime, David is most remembered with two brief passages of scripture: that he was a man after God's own heart (1 Samuel 13:14), and at the end of his life it was said that he had served God's purpose in his own generation (Acts 13:36). What a legacy! He became the measuring stick by which all of Israel's future kings were evaluated for over three centuries — not because of his military prowess, civil accomplishments, or building projects. The criterion by which all other kings were evaluated was whether or not they had served the Lord Jehovah like David had, with all of their hearts.

This section of our Bible study seeks to answer the question: "How did David become the man after God's own heart who was able to serve God's purposes in his generation?" David started out as just a boy with a sling who watched sheep. But God orchestrated events that changed him into the man he was to become. God wanted to build into David the characteristics of a tenderhearted warrior who could faithfully lead and protect his people. God can use this process in you as well, if you allow Him to. He specializes in taking stiff, selfish hearts and forever converting them into hearts that seek after God. Is God at work, using this process, in your life today?

As God's plan for David begins to unfold in this study, you will begin to discover His purposes for your life as well. This section of the workbook will lead you through the first third of a twelve-week excursion. When your journey ends, you will be forever changed. You will be ready and equipped to pursue God as David did, and you will be on your way to becoming a person after God's own heart.

David

An Old Prophet and a New King

As God calls us to use our gifts in His kingdom, He often creates a time of preparation before we are released into expanded influence over others. God does this so our character can catch up to our calling.

—John Dawson

Day One: Take a Look at God's Word

David's reign did not begin with the pomp and grandeur of a royal ceremony. His entry into the biblical landscape is obscured by the shadow of King Saul's decline, and takes place in the small village of Bethlehem. An onlooker might notice nothing more than a visit by an old prophet to a man's home for dinner. But God had great plans for this meeting.

Historically, the timing of this meeting occurred at roughly the midpoint of the reign of Israel's first king. King Saul had struggled to obey God. He had recently made several poor decisions and had not carried out God's commands; as a result, God called on an old servant and friend, the prophet Samuel, to quietly start a new chapter in Israel's history.

So our study into God's dealings with men's hearts begins as He calls the prophet Samuel to the task of finding God's next shepherd over His people.

Samuel served God his entire life. He had been a precious gift to a childless woman named Hannah decades earlier. Samuel's birth was a miracle, and Hannah dedicated his life back to God. When Samuel was old enough, he was brought to the temple to live and serve God. At this early age, God called him to be His messenger. Israel had slipped away from its first love, and Samuel would spend his lifetime restoring the kingdom's respect for the God who had made them a nation.

Read about Samuel's calling in 1 Samuel 3.

For whom did Samuel mistake God's voice? _____

_____

_____

Why do you suppose this was? _____

_____

_____

How did Eli tell Samuel to respond? _____

_____

_____

Have you had any mentors in your life, such as Eli was for Samuel? How have they influenced you to listen to and respond to God's voice?

_____

_____

_____

As the story continues, there are two specific points to note as God turns the corner in Israel's history and selects a new king.

Read 1 Samuel 15.

First, God was sorry He had selected Saul to be king. This harsh judgment was the result of a long pattern of Saul's faltering leadership, but the final straw was laid on the camel's back in this chapter.

What had happened?

_____

_____

Read 1 Samuel 16:14-16.

Why did God say He regretted making Saul king? (See chapter 15, verse 11.)

_____

_____

What are your thoughts about the change that has taken place in Saul's life?

_____

_____

Read 1 Samuel 16:1-13.

Second, God called Samuel to the specific task of finding and anointing a new king. This passage colors in the picture of a man, Samuel, who had spent his entire life walking with God. Samuel intimately knew God's voice, and God intimately knew him. The depth of this relationship is an incredible example of God's love for His people. He wants us to be as familiar with Him as we are with our own faces in the mirror!

God is not off in a distant corner of the universe, while we wander through our lives in bewilderment as to His existence. God constantly intersects with humankind, and this passage gives us a picture of His intimate interaction with His creation.

Knowing what you now know about David's background and future, can you see a purpose in the events of 1 Samuel 16:14-21? If so, what is it?

_____

_____

_____

Day Two: Samuel's Visit

"Samuel, Samuel." A still, small voice broke the morning quiet. Samuel stirred on his cot and rolled over, expecting to see a shadow in his tent's doorway. No one was there. "Samuel, Samuel," the quiet voice called again in the stillness of the early morning.

"Yes, Lord, I'm here."

Samuel thought back to the first time he had heard God's voice, as a child while lying on his mat in the temple. His God had called him that night, and through the years, Samuel had learned to recognize that Voice very well. He knew that he could trust the hand of God in his life. But as he rose to meet with God early this morning, Samuel prayed out loud, "O Lord, how many times have You whispered my name? I'm afraid these old bones don't rise quite as quickly as they did when I was young. But here I am, Lord. Send me."

The still, small voice called back: "Samuel, I want you to travel to Bethlehem. There is a family there whom I will show you. From this house, a new king over My people, Israel, will come." Samuel stilled himself as he considered the Lord's words.

"I'm Your servant, and I don't question You, but isn't that a little dangerous, Lord? Saul hasn't been the same since the battle with the Amalekites, when we confronted his disobedience at the battle's edge. I have heard of his anger, the spirits of rage that control him. Lord, I'm afraid. If I go, he will surely meet me on the way and kill me."

"Take a heifer from your flock and tell the people that you have come to sacrifice." The Lord hadn't seemed to hear Samuel's objections. And so Samuel rose immediately. He knew better than to argue with God's direction for his life.

The little town of Bethlehem sat in the green valley just to the west of the great Salt Sea. It could barely be called a town. Most of Bethlehem's residents had descended from a few Benjaminite families, and its only reason for existence was as a stopping place. Travelers found respite as they journeyed from the south end of the kingdom to the Jebusite town of Jerusalem, which lay a half day's journey to the north. Bethlehem rested in the shadow of Jerusalem, which David would later choose to be the center of Israel's public, political, and religious life. The news of Samuel's arrival stirred the entire town to life. Women hurried to get their laundry inside and make their children ready for the great prophet's visit. The marketers scurried to stock and open their carts. Surely this important traveler would want to refresh himself.

Samuel's status among the people was richly earned. He had served as God's leader and the voice of God for almost seventy years. Samuel had been the one to whom Israel had turned when they asked for a king. Samuel was still the one to whom Israel looked for spiritual guidance and to intercede to the Lord on their behalf.

The elders of the town met Samuel at the gate. They bowed low and said, "O Samuel, man of God, why is it you have come to our humble village? Is there some word from the Lord? Everything we have is yours. How can your servants please you today?"

"First of all," Samuel replied, "rise, rise. I am not a god but a man. I would like to meet with you in a man's house. His name is Jesse. I have come to sacrifice with him and his family." This seemed an odd request to the elders who had expected Samuel to sit in their synagogue and instruct them, but they didn't question the prophet. One hurried to find Jesse, and another to call his sons in from the fields. They scurried about like chickens in a courtyard, while Samuel was escorted by the third elder to Jesse's house.

As Samuel entered the small, dusty home, he noticed that it was well kept. Jesse's seven sons and wife were already assembled there. The eldest, Eliab, and the second born, Abinadab, were tall in stature. Samuel noticed they were fine young men. At their father's side before Samuel had even arrived, they assisted Jesse in gathering things for the meal. Their faces were dark and tanned for they had spent much time in the fields with their father's flocks. They shepherded the family's sheep under Jesse's guidance — one of these would surely make a fine king.

Jesse watched as Shimea, Nethanel, Raddai, and the two youngest sons all hurried about, one setting the table, another in the kitchen with his mother. One came in with a small animal to be a part of the sacrifice. But he didn't say a word when he noticed that Samuel had already brought his yearling heifer for the celebration. Under a gentle look from his father, Ozem quietly led the animal back outside. Eliab, the eldest, talked with his father. Samuel didn't catch the words, but the questioning looks on their faces led Samuel to believe that they were almost as confused about Samuel's presence in this house as was the prophet himself. Yet in the commotion, a quiet peace settled over Samuel's heart. He knew he was where God wanted him to be. He knew this was the home where Israel's next king would be found. As he rose to meet Jesse and be formally introduced to his sons, the peace of God's presence settled over Samuel and the entire home.

As Jesse's sons fell in line behind their father, from oldest to youngest, Samuel could see the relationships that framed this family. They honored their father as leader, example, and the gentle shepherd over their flocks and themselves, and they worked alongside him to provide for their large family. From youngest to oldest, each had learned under the shared yoke of responsibility. Above all, as Jesse began to introduce them, Samuel saw the unconditional acceptance that Jesse held for each of them. He saw this in the pride in Jesse's face as he called each of their names, and in the frames of his sons, who lifted themselves upright to bow low in respect to the old prophet. *Surely this is a fine home from which our next king will come*, Samuel thought.

"Samuel, we are honored to have you in our home. Let me introduce you to my sons. This is Eliab, my eldest." As Eliab passed before Samuel to greet him, Samuel thought, *What a fine, strong young man. Surely, Lord, this is the next king.*

God's Spirit quietly said, *No, Samuel, I do not look on a man as you do. I look at a man's heart, and this is not the one to lead My people.*

Next was Abinadab, much like his older brother, someone on whom his father relied to lead the sheep in and out of pasture, to protect and provide safety for them when it got cold and to see that the details of the family's herds were never neglected. But again, Samuel sensed that this was not the next leader of God's people. Next was Shimea. He was quite different from his older brothers. He seemed to have more of his mother's countenance and character. Samuel had noticed that as the family prepared for the meal, Shimea was the one who was in the kitchen with his mother, making sure she had all the supplies she needed. He had a compassion about him that was missing in his older brothers' strength, and Samuel thought again, *Surely, Lord, a man with a compassionate heart, a man from a strong family, surely this will be the kind of person who will lead Your people.*

But, once again, the Spirit of God whispered in Samuel's ear in a still, small voice, *No, this is not the one, Samuel.*

As Samuel met the next four sons, he still did not find the reason for his journey to Jesse's home. God's peace had not yet come to rest on any of these children. He blessed the youngest with his hand on the boy's shoulder. Samuel looked at Jesse and asked for them to pass in front of him again. *These bones are getting old, Lord, and so may be my hearing, Samuel prayed silently. Help Your servant to see which of these fine young men will lead Your children, Israel.* But again, the Spirit did not set apart any of Jesse's sons as the focus of Samuel's search.

Finally, after another silent prayer, Samuel turned to the patriarch. "Jesse, are these all of your children?"

There was an odd shuffling among Jesse and his family. Samuel did not understand their embarrassment. Jesse looked at his sons and said to the prophet, "No, Samuel, there is one more. He is in the field, tending the sheep."

Samuel settled in his chair and stated directly, "We will not continue until all of your children are here, Jesse." With a glance from Jesse, Ozem was out the back door, sprinting up the hillside to find his forsaken brother. Samuel was puzzled. Had he not said to Jesse that he was there to sacrifice and celebrate with his entire family? Had Jesse not been so proud of all of his sons? Why was this one any different? David's absence created more than one awkward question and an uncomfortable silence as they waited for the two sons to return.

Ozem quickly appeared in the back gate with his brother, and as this youngest one passed in front of Samuel, the Lord spoke clearly and plainly to his heart, *This is the one whom I have chosen. Anoint him, for he will be the next king of Israel.* Samuel gazed intently into this young man's eyes. He seemed different from the rest — quiet, almost timid. From the reaction of the older brothers as David came into the room, Samuel sensed that he wasn't very well liked, even an outcast. Eliab and Abinadab had a difficult time hiding the disdain from their faces as Samuel greeted their youngest brother. Maybe that was why this one was left in the fields. But understanding all of what God was doing…well…Samuel had given up on that long ago. He knew his God's voice, and he knew he could trust where Jehovah led. So as Samuel reached for the flask of oil at his side, he prayed quietly for the Spirit of the Lord to fill and baptize David in courage, strength, and wisdom.

What does God's choice for the next king of Israel say to you?

_____

_____

Write out 1 Samuel 16:7.

_____

_____

What is most important in God's eyes?

_____

Read verses 12 and 13. How does this scripture describe David?

_____

_____

When Samuel anointed David, what happened? How long did the Spirit of the Lord remain on David?

_____

These events illustrate the first of thirteen principles we will uncover — principles that God uses to mold and change our hearts.

Principle One: We meet God, begin a personal relationship with Him, and receive a personal revelation of His love for us.

Our lives must be open and tender before they can be usable in God's kingdom, as was David's. God's call and anointing often comes when we least expect it, sometimes even when we don't feel completely ready to step out into the path to which God calls us.

Not only was David a young man, fourteen or fifteen years old at the time of Samuel's visit, but the current king of Israel, Saul, was still years away from vacating the throne. But God chose this day to begin the process of molding within this young boy the heart that would empower him to become Israel's greatest king. David's rise to the throne was a journey and a process, and his anointing by Samuel was just the beginning.

Day Three: Who Was David?

David was the youngest in a family of many children, and from the few glimpses we gain from the historical biblical record, it seems he wasn't well received by his siblings, and possibly even by his father, Jesse. He was the baby of the family, and as in many large families, the older siblings held a unique disdain for the last in line. But this typical sibling rivalry between David and his older brothers does not explain the burning question that is left unanswered after Samuel left Jesse's house.

Why was David left in the fields tending sheep when the entire family had been summoned by the prophet to a sacrifice and worship celebration? Samuel was the spiritual leader of the entire nation of Israel. His presence in such a small town stirred the entire village to its feet. But Jesse deliberately left David out of the meeting. Why?

From your reading of these events, propose an answer to this question below.

_____

_____

_____

_____

_____

This event could be compared to a family's being granted an audience with the president of the United States, and then leaving one sibling out, not even telling him of the honor. Just a few chapters later in this string of events, Jesse called David to take supplies to his brothers in the battlefield. At that time, David left the sheep with the hired hands to carry out his father's desires (see 1 Samuel 17:20). So why had David been left alone, single-handedly tending his father's herds, when hired help was available?

While they might not be explicit in the biblical historical record, we can use these events to uncover some aspects of David's character. From David's interaction with his family members here and in later chapters, David seems to have been a bit of an outcast, a singular young man without many close family ties. Yet God specifically chose this young man to become a king.

Think of the times when you may have felt alone, left "out of the loop." What does this passage of scripture say to you about how God views the lonely?

_____

_____

_____

_____

In the next chapter, David would meet Goliath and take his first step toward Israel's throne — but he had been unknowingly preparing for that moment all of his life. (See 1 Samuel 17:34-37.) David may have been the youngest of many brothers, but we can see from the risks he took protecting his father's herds, he was loyal, fearless, and fiercely devoted to the tasks given him. His approach to life was decidedly different than those around him, and those qualities would serve him well as he ascended to the throne.

Your character is a product of the choices you make, and the reaction you have toward the circumstances in your life. David's situation and family relationships could have created a young man with little confidence or courage. But instead, David chose to become a young man who was not afraid to stand up for his convictions, even if his decisions created great personal risk.

David knew his God personally, but this relationship was significantly different from the understanding of Jehovah that was held by the Israelites. David's people culturally placed God in a position that was far away, cloistered behind thick royal curtains in the temple. God was Someone whom only priests could approach under the covering of elaborate ceremonies and holy clothing. David's perception was vastly different; he understood God to be his personal Protector and Provider. David wrote words to heaven, identifying the Lord God as a Friend to the friendless, a Father to the fatherless, and a High Tower to which he could run in times of trouble. David's perception of God was unique, intimate, and familial. Maybe this is a part of what God saw when He told Samuel that He had found a "man after My own heart."

As we look at David, we are spending a considerable amount of time identifying the starting point of his journey to the throne — and for good reason. Our discovery of the person David became is filled with valuable lessons only when we understand where he had come from.

Before we continue, take a minute and consider your own starting point. What is your perception of God? What are some of the events in your life that have shaped this viewpoint?

_____

_____

_____

_____

_____

_____

Remember, we are who we are based on our own reactions to situations. Begin today to frame your picture of God based on who He really is, not through the lenses of your circumstances.

Day Four: Yearning for God in a Dry and Thirsty Land

Personal courage and an intimate view of God — these two distinct characteristics are inexorably linked to each other in David's life.

David lived on the outer rim of his family ties, without the support of his father and brothers. In response, David became a young man who fended for himself, courageous, not afraid to take risks. David also lived on the edge of the comfort that intimate family relationships would have provided. To fill this vacuum, David found comfort in an intimate relationship with the living God. He learned to look to heaven and trust the God of his fathers.

Only God could have known the heart of this young man. God watched him keep his father's sheep, and God gave him the courage to fend off the wild animals. God must have sent special comfort on cold nights when David was the only one in the fields, thinking of his family at home asleep in their warm beds. From these experiences, David became a young man who yearned for more than what he had, and he learned to look to heaven to find the supply for those desires.

David wrote these lines in one of his most well-known psalms: *As the deer pants for streams of water, so my soul pants for you, O God* (Psalm 42:1).

Take a few minutes and review the details we have uncovered from David's life; then read Psalm 42. What image do you have of David? Draw up your own character sketch of this young man.

_____

_____

If you or I had met David during this time of his life, what would we have seen? Would we have seen a man after God's own heart, or an awkward adolescent? Would we have seen the honor, strength, and integrity that God had personally molded into his character?

Before we go on, take a few minutes and ask these questions of yourself: What is God doing in my life right now? What does God want to do in my life? How can I find courage, confidence, and faith in the difficult-to-understand events that may come into my life?

If your answer to these questions is, "I don't know," then write that below. But if you have a sense of the answers, either vague or specific, write your thoughts below. This is your starting point, the place from which you will journey on to discover God's heart and desire for your life.

_____

_____

_____

_____

_____

_____

_____

As we will soon see, Samuel's visit to David's home was the beginning of a new direction, but it was not a peaceful path that lay ahead for the young king. You might expect that if a man were to become a powerful king, he would need to be in the company of leaders, priests, and counselors who could teach him the skills he would need. David needed to be taught how to be an effective leader, but God trained him in unusual ways. His next years would be filled with both triumph and difficulty. He would build friendships, only to be betrayed. But David would find solace in difficult times in the hands of the One whom, he would learn, would never desert him.

Consider your own relationship with God. What do you want God to do in your life? What are some of the prayers you are hoping God will answer? How do you suppose God will prepare you for the future events of your life?

_____

_____

_____

_____

_____

_____

Day Five: Starting Your Journey with God

You may have been raised in a church with a lifetime of religious training and heritage, or you may have discovered God in your later years. But every person comes to a point in his life when he begins to follow Christ, when he makes a personal and deliberate choice to make an obedient relationship with Jesus his first priority.

Nicodemus had been raised in the faith and had become a leader in the Israelite religious community. Even though he knew the Scriptures and had obeyed the Law his entire life, Jesus still said to him, "I tell you the truth, no one can see the kingdom of God unless he is born again" (see John 3:3-7). Paul preached to the Philippian prisoners and jailer, *"Believe in the Lord Jesus, and you will be saved — you and your household"* (Acts 16:31). It's not important whether you have attended church your whole life or if you just heard the gospel message, there is a personal meeting God wants to have with you to offer you the opportunity to begin a new, born-again change in your life's direction.

John the Baptist, Jesus, and His disciples all preached the same message: *"Repent!"* (see Matthew 3:2, Mark 1:15, and Acts 2:38). They repeated the cry of Isaiah hundreds of years before: *"Let the wicked forsake his way and the evil man his thoughts. Let him turn to the LORD, and he will have mercy on him"* (Isaiah 55:7). They proclaimed this to both the Israelites and to the Roman soldiers who came to listen. There is a point in time when God meets each one of us, as He did in David's life when Samuel arrived in his house.

Describe the time in your life when you had a personal introductory meeting with God. Some call this being "born again" or receiving Christ. Whatever term you use to identify your decision to follow Christ and trust Him for your salvation, describe the events below.

_____

_____

_____

_____

_____

It may be that you have not yet made a conscious decision to follow Christ and make Him the focal point in your life. God's plan for salvation has four specific steps.

1. Repent.

Repentance is a change of heart, mind, and action. Repentance is a choice to leave your selfish ways behind and to follow a new direction into God's kingdom.

2. Believe.

Salvation is a gift. You can't earn it by good works, desires, or intentions. John 3:16 tells us that God so completely loved this world — including you — that He sent His only Son, Jesus, to us. Whoever believes in Him, believes that Jesus sacrificed His life as payment for their sins, will have eternal life.

3. Confess.

First John 1:9 tells us that if we confess our sins, God is faithful and just to forgive our sins and purify us from all unrighteousness. There is no "magic" involved in confessing your sins and receiving forgiveness, but you must acknowledge responsibility for your sins. By accepting the responsibility for our rebellious actions, we pave the pathway to receive God's forgiveness.

4. Receive.

By receiving Christ, you acknowledge that He has heard your prayers, forgiven your sins, and entered your life to give you the power and strength to follow His will. John 1:12 says, *To all who received him, to those who believed in his name, he gave the right to become children of God.*

If you have not yet made this decision to change the direction of your life, I invite you to pray this prayer to your heavenly Father:

> *Father God,*
>
> *I come to You in Jesus' name, recognizing that I have sinned and fallen short of Your glory. I confess to You that I have followed my own selfish desires for too long. Father, I believe that Your Son, Jesus, gave His life as payment for my sins, and that I can be forgiven because He rose from the dead and is now seated with You in heaven.*

Father God, please forgive me and come into my life. Jesus, I choose to make You my Lord, and I ask You to be my Savior. Grant me that courage and personal strength to obey You and give You first place in my life from this day forward. In Jesus' name. Amen.

If you have prayed this prayer for the first time, or felt the need to rededicate your life to Christ, I urge you to contact us at the address listed on the final pages of this book. We have a booklet we would like to send to you that will help you during the first month of your walk with Christ. And with your permission, we will find other believers in your area who can help you become a part of the family of God.

Week One: Summary

But the LORD said unto Samuel, Look not on his countenance, or on the height of his stature; because I have refused him: for the LORD seeth not as man seeth; for man looketh on the outward appearance, but the LORD looketh on the heart.

—1 Samuel 16:7 KJV

This week's lessons have introduced you to David and the ways in which God worked in his life. What is one new idea that you have learned this week? If there is one thought or idea which God used to grab your attention, write it on the lines below.

_____

_____

_____

_____

_____

_____

_____

_____

_____

_____

_____

_____

David

Faithful Friends and Unexpected Events

Humility is taught
by hardship in the face of obedience.
Humility is tested
by the choices we make.

Day One: Take a Look at God's Word

As we read through the pages of David's life, it is easy to miss the time frame in which these events took place. The process God used to mold a desert shepherd boy into a king and military champion spanned more than two decades. First Samuel chapters 17 through 20 tell of God's beginning this process. Take the time to imagine yourself standing with David under the desert sun. What would it be like to face Goliath, having never before been in battle? How would you respond to the personal friendship extended to you by King Saul and his son? Would you continue to trust God even as the mountaintop of victory suddenly gave way to the valley of injustice?

Read through these chapters in a quiet, restful place, and consider how and why God would use events like these to prepare a man to be king.

Record your thoughts below.

Chapter 17

_____

_____

_____

_____

_____

Chapter 18

_____

_____

_____

_____

_____

Chapter 19

_____

_____

_____

_____

_____

Chapter 20

_____

_____

_____

_____

_____

Day Two: David, Saul, and Jonathan

David stood uneasily in the entry to the royal tent, Saul's field office for the forty-day-old campaign against the Philistines. *I've been here before, he thought. Years ago I sat over there and played for Saul when he was afflicted with his violent moods.* As the swords clashed and the war cries rose from the battlefield outside, David shifted his weight from one foot to the other. He wasn't in Saul's presence as a servant today. He'd been summoned as a champion and a hero of the Israelite army.

"Come, come forward, my young champion," called Saul from the inner alcove. "Come and receive your reward for your bravery. You have wrought God's people a mighty victory today."

David emptied his arms in the front corner of the tent. The blood-covered sword was almost half his height. David had dragged it from the battle along with Goliath's shield. They smelled of the Philistine warrior, and both were a sign of David's victory and the Philistine's death.

He entered slowly and bowed low before Saul. "My king, your servant is here only to wait upon you and to serve God. What I have done today is what any soldier would do, to bring victory to our land and to deliver this Philistine dog into the armies of the living God. I seek no other reward, O king."

As David bowed, he reflected on his first meeting with Saul. A few months after the old prophet had anointed David, a second visitor from Jerusalem had called on Jesse's home looking for someone who was skilled on the harp. David loved to write music, and he often played to his flock on the hillside. During cool evenings, David's melodies echoed through the trees. Neighboring shepherds could hear the young boy playing to his God, and news of David's talents had traveled among the herdsmen.

Word had traveled as far as Jerusalem. When the king sent to find a skilled musician to help soothe his emotions, David was summoned to the king's courtyard. David played whenever Saul was troubled, and a bond had formed between the two — the watcher of sheep and the shepherd of God's people. David played the sweet songs he had written, and as he did, the peace of God returned to Saul. The monarch grew to treasure his young friend and soon made David his armor bearer. Before battle, David would bring the king his bronze breastplate, shield, and sword. Later, David would greet the weary king after a long campaign, return his armor to its mountings on the wall, and then play again for the moody monarch as Saul went about his daily duties.

David served the king for over a year, and Saul grew quite fond of the boy. When the king finally overcame his bouts with anger and dark depression, he thanked the boy for his service, blessed him, and sent him back to his father's house.

On this day, however, Saul didn't immediately recognize David. David's stature was strong and true, and today he had stood between the armies of Israel and a warrior twice his size, Goliath of Gath.

"You can't say that about my God!" David was the only one who answered Goliath's taunts. "For forty days you have blasphemed the armies of the living God. He is mighty. He is true. He is alive. And today He will deliver you into my hands!" David's words had echoed across the plains. In David's mind, the outcome of this confrontation was as sure as the sunrise. How else would the living God defend His people and chase this Philistine from their land?

Now, David bowed before King Saul. As Saul spoke, David stood upright and received the king's praise. The king invited David to be a part of his court, his army, and his family. Looking David squarely in the eye, he said, "You are a man in whom I see God working mightily. The God of our fathers has chosen you to lead His people." Saul did not realize the prophetic nature of his words. "So this day, my young warrior, you will enter my service. You may marry my daughter and lead a garrison of 1,000 men. They respect you and will remember your victory here for many years. God will work through your hands to chase the Philistines from our land."

At Saul's right hand stood his young son, Jonathan. Although similar in age and stature to David, Jonathan had been raised in the king's household. His hands had never birthed a sheep on a cold desert night. His face had never endured the harsh rays of the midday sun. David could tell by his delicate frame that he had never climbed the rocks searching for a goat that had wandered off, nor swam in a crystal-blue stream on a lazy afternoon. Yet Jonathan looked at David and saw someone whom he admired and trusted, someone with whom he would build a deep and abiding friendship.

The prince stepped forward under Saul's approving nod and said, "This day you have brought a mighty victory to God's people. As a reward, I would like to give you a treasure of my own." Jonathan removed his sword, his armor, and his outer royal robe and handed them to David. "In remembrance of this day, and as a sign of my friendship with you, please accept these gifts."

David stepped backward. "Who am I that I should accept such a wonderful gift from the king's family? I'm merely a servant of God — and of you. I have done nothing of great merit today."

At Jonathan's insistence, however, David relented. He reached for the gifts from the king's young son, but then quickly retracted his arms as he realized they were still covered in the Philistine's blood. Saul motioned for his cupbearer to come with a basin of water. As he cleansed the blood of the Philistine from his hands and arms, David realized that he was initiating a new chapter in his young life. This day his life had changed. He was no longer the youngest son in a large family, the keeper of his father's sheep, from the small town of Bethlehem. Today, David stepped into leadership in the king's army. This was not something he had sought for himself, but it was a blessing foreshadowed by Samuel's visit many years ago. He gratefully accepted Jonathan's gifts, and with them, David symbolically accepted the gift of God's anointing to follow King Saul in succession to the throne.

The following months were filled with praise and tribute. Saul led his army back into Jerusalem after each military triumph. Crowds on both sides of the street shouted and cheered. Women looked for their husbands, and young ladies gawked at the young, strong men fresh from the battlefields. David rode close beside Jonathan — not in the ranks with the common soldiers, but on a camel with the captains, toward the head of the column. Word of David's bravery often traveled to Jerusalem far ahead of the returning troops, and the people shouted praises to David as well as to Saul: "Praise be to Saul, who has killed his thousands, and to David, who has killed his ten thousands."

At the sound of these words from the crowd, David couldn't quite believe his ears, still uneasy with his new position. As the column neared the king's palace, Saul glanced back and found David in the procession. His eyes met David's with furtive displeasure. Was it jealousy that cast its shadow across the king's face?

David began to lead many victorious campaigns against the Philistines to the south and east and returned to many growing celebrations. While in the palace, David again played for the king, whose despondency was returning. But his friendship with the king gradually shifted. Saul watched David and Jonathan's friendship deepen, and the green eyes of jealousy often clouded his vision. David and Jonathan spent hours talking, walking through the marbled palace halls. They met in the royal stables, cared for their animals together, and prepared for battles in days to come. The more time they spent together, the closer they became.

David had yearned for a friend like this. Seeing Jonathan walking through the dusty stable one day, he caught up to him and asked, "Jonathan, my friend, I was raised with seven brothers, but none of them treated me with the kindness of you and your father. What have I done to deserve your favor?"

Jonathan's simple reply released a peace that David had known only on the day of Samuel's visit. "David, I feel as though you are the brother I never had. You are now the leader that I was born to be, and the champion that I may yet become. You are my friend. I honor your service to my father. I see God working to deliver our people through your hands."

As David and Jonathan's friendship deepened, so did Saul's depression. He wrestled unseen demons, grappling with them for his own emotional control. David was called more frequently to play his harp, and it seemed that his duties to lead his regiment of soldiers sometimes interfered with the king's desire to have David sit and play for hours. As David sat in Saul's presence one afternoon, Saul's menacing unnerved him. Saul's armor bearer and cupbearer were asked to leave the room. When only David and the king remained, Saul lunged for the javelin that rested in a golden vase beside his throne.

"You!" Saul cried out. "You intend to steal this throne from my son. I won't have it!" Before David could even move, the javelin was in the air and glanced off the wall just over his left shoulder. A shower of marble fragments sprayed against David's tunic. As Saul fumbled for another spear, David disappeared out the doorway. He dropped his harp in the hall and sprinted for the stables. Looking back over his shoulder, he expected to see the king. But no one saw David flee that day; no one had seen him escape the king's chambers. No one knew, and hours later, even David was left wondering what exactly had occurred.

Two days passed, and once again David was called to minister to the king's malaise. The king was like a different man. *Has he forgotten the events of just a few days ago?* David wondered. *Am I safe here?* He looked toward heaven as he entered the king's court. *Jehovah-Jireh, my Provider, my Shield and High Tower, the One to whom I run when I am in trouble, I trusted You when I saved the lambs from the bear. And You protected me as I chased the lion through the forest to redeem the sheep he had stolen. Lord, You stood with me on the battlefield with Goliath. Yet I have never before stood in danger from someone whom I have called my friend. Lord, protect me this day! I trust in You.*

David entered Saul's court and began playing, but the king's countenance grew darker instead of brighter. He glared at David and again asked his servants to leave. Yet again David fled the king's wrath and his sword, but this time David determined not to return.

He drifted through the courtyard in a daze, then through the stables. As dusk fell, he realized that the places he was drawn to were those where he and Jonathan had spent so much of their time together. Had Jonathan also turned his friendship into hatred? Would he turn on him as well? But the next day when David was not at the king's table, Jonathan came looking for him. He found David beneath one of their favorite trees in a field far from the palace. As they talked, David unloaded the previous day's events on his comrade.

David now feared for his life while in the king's presence. As the hours of conversation passed, Jonathan realized that God had selected David as the next king of Israel. Although it should have been Jonathan's birthright, God was instead preparing this young shepherd to lead Israel into the future. Jonathan looked at David and said solemnly, "Promise me this. When you lead our people, do not let your favor depart from my house. Promise me that you will watch over my descendants to the third and fourth generations." They wept on each other's shoulders as David committed his faithfulness to this true friend.

They made a plan for the next day, and as night closed in, David found a place to curl up under their favorite tree. David thought back to the countless days and nights that he had spent in the fields with his father's sheep. The smell of the dew on his clothes, and the tree root under his head...these images were still a part of David's identity. But as the events of the past few years passed through his mind, they seemed discontinuous: herding sheep, Samuel's anointing, playing the harp for the king as a boy, the defeat of Goliath, and becoming a warrior in the Israelite army. And now he was a fugitive, hiding in the fields and fearing for his life!

The only unbroken thread woven through his adolescence and early adulthood was Jehovah, his Friend, Protector, and God. In triumph and tragedy, David knew that God was at his side. For David, this wasn't knowledge that was simply learned in a temple on a Sabbath. David had lived these lessons as he learned them, but now this lesson was becoming painful. David finally found a shallow sleep, singing to himself in the same way that he used to sing to his sheep: *Why are you cast down, O my soul? And why are you disquieted within me? Hope in God; For I shall yet praise Him, The help of my countenance and my God* (Psalm 42:11 NKJV). He didn't have any more answers, but David knew the One who did.

The next day, Jonathan met David and confirmed his fears regarding Saul's plot. They talked. They wept. David had no further options but to leave Jerusalem. *What have I done? he wondered. What have I done to bring the king's wrath on me? Father in heaven, why are these things happening to me?* As David looked back at Jonathan, he remembered their vow one more time. Jonathan returned to the city, and David scurried into the evening dusk toward Nob. Ahimilech the priest was there, an old friend of his father. If there was any place David could find help, it would be in the house of God.

For his years of service, David had been rewarded with a powerful and psychologically unstable enemy. He was tempted to respond the same way toward Saul as the king had behaved toward him. *It would be so simple,* David thought, *to return tonight to Jerusalem and rally the troops. They must see the inevitable demise of the king. I've witnessed the troops' dissatisfaction with Saul's leadership — and they would follow me. It would be a small thing to eliminate the king. After all, the people also took to me as their leader.* But as David entertained these thoughts, the Spirit of God overwhelmed him. God's presence seized him as if by the arm, and David stopped in his tracks. David felt the Lord's displeasure at his ponderings.

You will not touch my anointed, God seemed to say.

That was enough for David, and the only sound breaking the cool desert night was the stones under his feet as he hastened to find the priest at Nob.

Does Saul's treatment of David seem unfair to you? Why?

_____

_____

_____

_____

Place yourself in Jonathan's shoes. How might you have responded when faced with the knowledge that God intended another person — your friend — to take your rightful place of honor?

_____

_____

_____

List some of the qualities in David's character that you see demonstrated in this story. Are any of these qualities present in your own character? Why or why not?

_____

_____

_____

_____

Day Three: The Sculptor Prepares His Clay

Have you ever been in a situation at work or in some other relationship in which you were treated unfairly or in some other way that left you feeling somehow inferior or second-rate? Maybe you were passed over for a well-deserved promotion, or a personal relationship may have unraveled. With over half of the marriages in our country ending in divorce (both inside and outside of the church), it is very likely that you or someone close to you has been touched by this tragic situation. Our lives are not usually a constant dismal stream of difficulty and despair, but when injustice and suffering do come, how do we respond? Where can we find comfort? What is God up to when He allows the shadow of tragedy to fall across our paths?

These events in David's life that we considered yesterday took place a few years after he was initially anointed by Samuel as the next king of Israel. During this time, he was first a shepherd in his father's home, and then he became the armor bearer and personal bard for King Saul. Later, he became a military champion and a leader of the armies of Israel. And then, suddenly, David was persecuted, forced to flee for his life as an outlaw. He was forced to leave behind everything he knew in order to seek refuge in the fields and forests outside of the cities.

Last week, we learned that David was most likely the overlooked youngest son in a large family. But now, after having tasted recognition and success, he was suddenly returned to that outcast lifestyle by events beyond his control. This time he was hunted by the one he'd called a friend, the one with whom he'd initially found acceptance. In David's life, God moved to prevent his rising star of influence from eclipsing the God who is the Bright and Morning Star over all creation. The trials which David would face throughout the next years were not mere short-term inconveniences, but God used them to forge the foundation of character in this leader for over a decade. These events illustrated the second principle in the divine character-building process.

Principle Two: God provides the opportunity for a period of initial peace, victory, or success, but then He shapes your life through circumstances, events, or other people.

During the first part of this principle, everything seems positive, and your walk with God seems to flourish unimpeded. In David's life, change did not take place immediately after Samuel anointed him as the next king of Israel. He returned to tending his father's herds. He still had a rotten relationship with his brothers. He still was the baby of the family with all the perks and scorn that position brought him. But something was different in David's heart. David became fearless as he protected his father's sheep, single-handedly rescuing one from a lion and another from a bear.

David also found time to write psalms, poems from his heart to the living God who had become personal and very real to him. This time of growth happened *prior to* David's public victory over Goliath. During this time, David also gained recognition in King Saul's court. He was invited to play for the king as Saul's periods of depression became more frequent. This time of "victory" in David's life progressed relatively unimpeded, as David advanced from one positive event to another, learning to see the hand of God at work in his life.

In your own Christian experience, this period can be compared to a time in which you personally grew in your faith and confidence in your relationship to God. Some call this period in a Christian's life "being discipled," or "growing in grace."

Think about a time of victory, peace, or success in your own Christian life. Describe this period on the lines below.

_____

_____

_____

_____

_____

_____

_____

_____

_____

How did this particular time in your life relate to your commitment or personal experience with God?

_____

_____

_____

_____

What are some of the events you can remember, or the Scriptures that were personally meaningful to you during this time?

_____

_____

_____

_____

_____

_____

_____

_____

What did you learn about God, His relationship to you, and His care for you during this time?

_____

_____

_____

_____

_____

_____

_____

_____

_____

_____

Day Four: Forming the Image of Christ

During the time of peace you considered in yesterday's lesson, God builds your trust in Him and then gradually arranges the circumstances that He will use to form your character. In David's life, his relationship with God was already firmly established before he faced the crisis with King Saul. Some of the circumstances in your own life may involve old friends, or a new circle of friends who are on a similar path, who can provide you with encouragement and camaraderie as you learn to walk out your faith. These three tools — personal trust in God, true friends, and difficult circumstances — are used in the hands of a skillful Artist to create Christ-like character out of our selfishness. When something goes terribly wrong, plummeting us into frustration or grief, God introduces a further insight into principle two of the process of forging Christ-likeness. God personally moves events to purify the motives and intents of our hearts.

Principle Two (elaborated): God shapes your life through circumstances, events, or other people. Through true friends, false alliances, and suffering injustice or other hardships, He sculpts Christ-like character into our selfish hearts. This process can be painful, but the final result is that we become more like Jesus.

What friends, mentors, or new comrades did God bring into your life during the early years of your Christian faith?

_____

_____

Did any of your friends or family members not understand the new direction in your life? Were there people who did not share your new priorities?

_____

_____

Events such as these rarely are as drastic as what we have seen take place in David's life, yet your character will be shaped by the difficulties you face that draw you closer to God, and that distance you from a life outside of His influence.

Were there events like these in your life? If so, what happened, and how did you react?

_____

_____

_____

_____

_____

Did any of your friends, new or old, create situations that seemed unfair or unjust?

_____

_____

_____

Looking back at these events, how did you respond, and what lessons did you learn? What did you learn about yourself, and about God?

_____

_____

_____

_____

Did these events increase your faith and your trust in God? Do you still struggle with bitterness or unforgiveness regarding what took place? Are there any remnants of negative thoughts or feelings from these experiences that you are still clinging to, things that God may now want you to reconsider, grow from, and release to Him? Write your final thoughts on the lines below.

_____

_____

_____

_____

_____

_____

_____

_____

Day Five: In the Hands of God

In many maturing Christians' lives, there comes a time when God allows everything they hold dear to drift away, leaving them with only His Presence on which to rely. If this occurs in your life, you're not alone! During the times when God seems far away, not only is He nearer than you can imagine, but He is specifically working in your life to create a treasure beyond measure.

Do you know the difference between a diamond and a lump of coal? Other than what you would pay for each, the only difference between these two pieces of stone is time and pressure. Diamonds are formed out of ordinary pieces of coal which are kept in a state of high pressure deep in the earth for a long period of time. When unexplained or unjust difficulty finds its way into your life, cling to the Rock that will remain steadfast during the storm. The choices you make during such times are those that will change you forever.

Physical fitness trainers tell us that muscles are built up by the process of overcoming progressive resistance. Our muscles attain greater strength after they are used to lift, move, run, or otherwise undergo active use. In the process, the muscle is actually broken down and damaged by the use. As muscle tissue regrows to repair the area, nature overcompensates and builds more muscle in order to prepare for the next expected use.

In order to take on the image of Christ, your character must also endure a process of pressing on against difficulties. By overcoming opposition and choosing to remain faithful in the face of temptation or injustice, we burn off added pounds of selfishness and take on the fitness profile of heaven itself: a Christ-like character.

Looking back over the responses you have given this week, is there a major theme, or central thought, that runs through your entries? In what way has this lesson applied to your personal Christian walk? How will you apply this lesson to your life?

Write your thoughts below.

_____

_____

_____

_____

_____

_____

_____

This final step may be the most difficult. The process used throughout this study is one of application toward personal change, and this process has three distinct steps.

1. Learning
2. Reflection
3. Application

Learning is the information-gathering stage. You are exposed to facts and information to engage your mind and heart. The journaling you do helps you to reflect and begin to understand this new information in the light of your own personal history. Journaling is a reflective approach to begin to apply the knowledge to your own habits and beliefs. But in order for the lesson to have lasting influence on your life, there must also be application. Application includes a change in your personal actions that effects permanent change in your life. Through application you build new habits based on the learning and reflection you have done. And changing a life is not an easy course of action.

Throughout this lesson, you have been slowly led toward applying God's truth and participating in God's will for your life. Personal change is not an easy course of action, and it can be a bit frightening after years of living with old, comfortable habits. So let's take the process one small step at a time.

Looking back at the personal insights you have identified in your journaling, identify one specific facet of your life that "sticks out" in your mind more than any other.

What one idea or personal revelation has made the most impact on your study this week?

_____

_____

_____

Based on this one idea, what specific action can you take during this next week to apply this lesson to your life? You may want to write these thoughts in the form of a to-do list, if that fits your style, or in the form of a prayer to God.

_____

_____

_____

_____

_____

_____

Father in heaven,

 I desire to take on Your character and become a person whom You can use and through whom Your Holy Spirit can flow. In David's life, You used his friends, both true and feigned, as well as difficulties and triumphs, to mold his heart into Your own character.

 Father, sculpt my own heart, forge my character, and polish my being so that I can reflect Your image to everyone I encounter.

 In Jesus' name. Amen.

Week Two: Summary

Truly the light is sweet, and a pleasant thing it is for the eyes to behold the sun: But if a man live many years, and rejoice in them all; yet let him remember the days of darkness; for they shall be many.

—Ecclesiastes 11:7-8 KJV

This week's lessons have introduced you to some new ideas about David and the ways in which God worked in his life. What is one new idea that you have learned this week? If there is one thought or idea that God used to grab your attention, write it on the lines below.

_____

_____

_____

_____

_____

_____

_____

_____

_____

_____

_____

_____

_____

David

WEEK THREE

Making Choices with God's Guidance

As for me, I will call upon God; and the LORD
shall save me.

—Psalm 55:16 KJV

Day One: Take a Look at God's Word

David spent the next few years of his life on the run — hunted by Saul like a desert coyote. Saul's moodiness and contempt for David grew. In his consuming paranoia, Saul eventually sought to kill David, fearing that he would eventually take the throne from his family. Almost overnight, David had been reduced from a military hero to a political fugitive, and this period of David's life spanned more than ten years.

Justice? Fairness? These notions were driven from David's experience like Saul's chariot wheels slicing through the parched desert sand. After having tasted success and acceptance for the first time in his young life, David now fled in fear. He had done nothing wrong, but yet he now held no power over his own destiny. These events seemed to create an ominous portrait of David's future, and he could not see when, or how, the final brush strokes would be applied.

This week's readings are found in 1 Samuel 23 through 26. Although some of these stories may seem familiar to you, these events are rarely found in popular sermon topics. Take some time to thoughtfully read these chapters. Look for any familiar passages, and jot down your thoughts below. Over the next several days, we will revisit these passages, and more closely examine these four major events: the battle at Ziph, the oasis at En Gedi, David's encounter with Nabal and Abigail, and his final test at Hachilah.

For each of the following events, describe what takes place and any lessons that can be learned from the incident.

The Battle at Ziph

_____

_____

_____

The Oasis at En Gedi

_____

_____

_____

David's Encounter with Nabal and Abigail

_____

_____

_____

David's Test at Hachilah

_____

_____

_____

Day Two: David's Circumstances — God's Molding Furnace

David's Environment

The arid countryside through which David wandered encompassed roughly 120 square miles. Imagine driving a car on any major highway for forty miles in a straight line. Then take the area you traversed and draw boundary lines one-and-a-half miles to one side, and one-and-a-half miles on the other side. You've constructed a rectangular area approximately three miles wide and forty miles long, which defines the area in which David and his mercenaries took cover for the next decade. The landscape was hilly, rugged, unforgiving, and composed mostly of desert terrain. At times David hid in the cities on the Salt Sea (the modern-day Dead Sea), and during other seasons he sought refuge in the mountains, caves, and canyons near the shoreline. David wandered in the plains toward the west, approaching the Mediterranean Sea, or through the Philistine's region near Gath just to the south. He was forced to trust his future to Jehovah, as he made an ally of the adversarial terrain.

David's Companions

David's companions during this time were a group of mercenaries whose numbers grew steadily to nearly 600 men. These men were the outcasts from the cities that David visited. They found friendship with David and chose to cast their lot with him. Some of them were his cousins and relatives. Two, Abishai and Joab, would later become trusted generals during his reign, and they developed great loyalty to David during this time in the wilderness.

While God was working in David's life to create humility and leadership ability, these mercenaries were also being transformed into the core of David's army. These men would eventually be invaluable to the future success of David's military campaigns as he established Israel's borders.

There is a type of man who would rather find comfort running in the wilderness than building a furnished home. There is a certain disposition of character which leads him to seek solace with only a rock for a pillow and branches for warmth at night. These were

David's friends and his solitary community; they would rather live in the fields with a trusted outlaw-leader than in a city with family and friends.

When we think about these mercenaries, these professional soldiers, we think of men with coarse and hardened countenances. These men didn't sign on with David so they could see the world and "be all they could be." These men would rather fight than get along. They would rather pick up a weapon and defend a personal cause than stay home and build relationships with people that they could trust. A typical mercenary is fiercely loyal to the cause in which he believes, and often identifies that chosen battleground as part of himself. He is a man who is self-sufficient, who is very slow to pledge his allegiance to anyone. But on the other hand, he is a person who will be fiercely loyal to those whom he intentionally chooses to let inside his circle of influence.

These companions were drawn to David and became the corps of the military whom David trusted with his life, and whom he learned to lead. God used this time of hardship in David's life to not only prepare a king for a throne, but also to prepare those who would be the backbone of the Israelite army, and their preparation was just as crucial as that of their leader. In the upcoming years, David built the loosely knit Hebrew families into an economic and political power. His army was necessarily forged through the trial of this desert experience — along with David's character and leadership abilities. David's kingdom ushered in a Golden Age which he was later able to pass on to his son Solomon. Even though he was called a "man of blood" because he was a mighty warrior, David brought peace to all of Israel. And he could not have done that without the military — the army that willingly followed him from the fields and caves to the palace.

David's Allies

In the early years of his exile, David carefully built his group of allies. At that time, the Israelites were a nomadic people living in small tribes and villages scattered throughout the region. David needed a network of supporters in case King Saul ever were to catch him unprepared.

According to 1 Samuel, David selected opportunities to sell his mercenary services. After the long winters, neighboring nomadic tribes often raided Israel's outlying settlements. They descended on the farmers' flocks, took the best of the herd, and raided the granaries of leftover crops. The nomadic Bedouin shepherds did not have the reserves that a close-knit farming community offered, so the stronger raiders took what they needed from the more domestic Israelite farmers. David often encamped to defend outlying settlements that had little protection of their own. In return, he would receive food, clothing, and provisions for his men. The nomadic traditions of the Middle East made this practice customary among wandering tribes and the small settlements that dotted the hills and valleys of Israel at that time.

Thus David learned to live by his wits, even in the times when he did not face a direct assault by King Saul. This day-to-day existence was the canvas God selected on which to paint the background for the rest of David's life. Jehovah cultivated the colors, hues, and images of a man after his own heart through this difficult time, rather than in spite of it. And this leads us to the third principle that God uses to mold and change our hearts:

Principle Three: God's loving tests continue until we come to a place of utter dependence on Him. We learn to look to Him and behave in ways consistent with God's character, regardless of whatever injustice, trial, or opportunity for temporary personal gain comes our way.

How do you see principle three reflected in David's life?

_____

_____

_____

How can you see it reflected in your own?

_____

_____

_____

_____

Day Three: Encounters with King Saul

The Battle at Keilah

Read 1 Samuel 23:1-21.

One of the first skirmishes between Saul and David took place in Keilah, a small town in the hill country between the Mediterranean and Salt Seas. David and his men, some of whom were from Keilah, stood against the Philistines and inflicted heavy damage while defending the small city. They carried away much of the Philistine's livestock and then retreated to the hills. Doeg, an Edomite who managed Saul's men and household, received news of David's involvement in this battle, and he leaked David's location to the king. Saul immediately mounted a charge of 3,000 men to ferret David out of the wilderness. While they were resting in the hills just outside of Keliah, David's scouts became aware of Saul's approach, and they moved into cover in the wilderness forests of Ziph.

Two, maybe three, years had passed since David had been driven from the palace by Saul's rage. This first skirmish with Saul was a painful reminder of these events. But God personally brought David a messenger of hope in the middle of his trial. Even in the wilderness, God would provide divine encouragement and unexpected hope when David's own personal resources were depleted. Jonathan, David's friend and comrade, sought out David at this time in the wilderness of Ziph. Picture this meeting with me.

David was weary from battle and jaded by the constant flight. The reality that he might live this way for an undetermined length of time had just begun to settle in. Through the night darkness, Joab escorted Jonathan into the camp. Jonathan and David embraced, and the king's son affirmed the word of the Lord that David would be the next king over Israel. Unselfishly, he claimed no hope for the throne himself. The two encouraged each other for hours, walking through the wooded hillside and among the camels as they had when David walked the marble halls in Jerusalem. As the night hours grew long, Jonathan departed, ending the last meeting between these two great men.

David's nighttime visit with his friend unsettled his men. Around their campfires, the questions stirred. As the lamb slowly roasted on the fire, the subject of Jonathan's visit awkwardly surfaced in the conversation.

One elbowed his friend, "Hey, do you think David will be king?"

From across the fire, another growled, "If David is king, and we will be king's men, then what are we doing out in this desert?"

After a short silence, a third responded, "I don't believe it. It's just talk. I don't know who this visitor was, but why would Saul's son be a friend of David, if David will take his place on the throne?"

The men gazed into the crackling embers of their fire as the cold night air embraced them again. The unanswered question hung in the campfire's smoke, the question none of them could escape: "If we are serving a king, then why are we running like jackals through the woods?"

In Palestine, ascension to a throne by assassination was a commonplace event. Men often rose to positions of leadership by assassinating anyone who stood in their way. It was not atypical for a rival leader to put together a small army, like David's, slip into the royal chambers, and by morning emerge as the new king. But this was not David's way. It would not have been the way of a man after God's own heart to follow culturally acceptable actions when God's word pointed toward a different route. David believed God's promises, even though it meant enduring pain and suffering with no foreseeable end. David knew God, and he trusted God. That was enough for him.

Write your thoughts about David, and how his choices can be applied as an example in your life on the lines below.

_____

_____

_____

_____

_____

_____

The Oasis at En Gedi

Read 1 Samuel 23:22-24:22.

After the skirmish in the wilderness of Ziph, David and his men traveled east, across the desert of Moan, and found refuge in the oasis of En Gedi. A small valley a mile or so from the shores of the Salt Sea, En Gedi was a hidden haven of lush greenery and crystal clear waters. The centuries-old spring flowed down the face of the rock and coaxed succulent green vines and foliage into bloom. As the water struck the desert floor, it formed a small stream that flowed out the western shore of the Salt Sea. At the top of the steep cliffs that protected En Gedi's reclusive greenery, the barren desert stood as a silent sentinel, offering little cover for approaching enemy troops.

In the daytime, hot winds blew across the sands toward the Salt Sea. At night, foul breezes flowed back, carrying the stale stench of a sea in which nothing lived or grew. But God provided this cool green shelter to calm David's weary heart and refresh his men. At En Gedi, Saul once again stalked David, searching for him with 3,000 men. And it was here that David was given his first opportunity to ascend to the throne by his own means.

Scouts warned of Saul's approach, and David's men dispersed into the crags of the rock face. They hid toward the back of caves and along the walls, hoping that Saul's army would pass. But just at that moment, Saul too decided to refresh himself with a short nap. The 3,000-man column stopped, and Saul entered the very cave in which David and many of his closest men were hiding. What an opportunity! Or was it a test of the future king's heart? Some men looked at this as God's hand…Saul had been delivered to David — on a platter, no less. They whispered to David, "This is God's answer! The victory is yours, David. Take it!"

"No, I will not raise my hand against God's anointed," David replied. Saul may have been stumbling in and out of God's will as he sought to extinguish David's life, yet David knew that raising his hand against God's anointed king was not the right thing to do, regardless of how providential an opportunity it seemed to be. And so, David and his men stayed hidden until Saul left.

Although military strategy was not the apparent reason for David's restraint, his decision to spare King Saul demonstrated his growing leadership skills. Three thousand of the king's troops were positioned outside of the cave while Saul napped. If he hadn't come out, Saul's generals would have searched the cave, only to find the king in a pool of blood. Immediately, 3,000 troops would have descended on the caves to find the murderer, and David and his men would have been trapped like squirrels in a cage. It would have been foolish, not to mention suicidal, to kill Saul at that moment. David demonstrated his growing wisdom as he placed his men's well-being ahead of his own ambition.

Our life's most difficult seasons are those in which God works to carve godly character out of our carnal, selfish desires. Fraught with pitfalls, snares, and dead ends, this wilderness is a maze of injustice, difficult circumstances, or personal failure, in which we can sometimes get lost. But this desert injustice prepares our heart and forges our character. We may not understand, but we can choose our response. Difficult events can soften us and teach us God's mercy and grace, or they can harden our hearts with unforgiveness, backbiting, and fear. The choice is up to us.

How do you usually react to difficult circumstances in your life? Do you look for God's hand in the situation, or do you allow bitterness to take root?

_____

_____

_____

_____

_____

_____

_____

Some circumstances, like those David faced, are caused by the actions of others, over which we have absolutely no control. Yet they affect our lives just the same. Consider the instance of the Christian whose spouse decides that an active Christian life is no longer his or her desire. The result at best is a home in which quarrelsome parents wrestle over principles and priorities. At worst this setting can often find resolution in a painful and difficult divorce.

What about the boss who insists that his employees cut corners, use substandard materials, hedge on the facts, or take unnecessary risks? They are then faced with the choice of compromising their integrity or possibly losing their job. Or what about the decisions your children make? One drunk-driving incident, a teenage pregnancy, or casual drug use can change a young person's life forever. These events aren't relegated to outside the church's gates. They can sweep into anyone's life like a torrential Texas rainstorm. The raging waters cannot soak into the hard prairie soil, and so they have no other outlet than to sweep chaos into your life. But God can use these events to form your character, faith, and stability in dark and difficult times.

What about you? Can you describe events like these when other people's choices negatively affected your life?

_____

_____

_____

What was your reaction to these events? What happened to change the situation?

_____

_____

What have you learned from the example of David's life and God's faithfulness to him in difficult circumstances? How can you specifically look for God to walk alongside of you during your difficult times?

_____

_____

_____

_____

If there are events such as these in your life today, what do you believe God would have you do? Write one or two specific action points below that you believe would introduce God's redemptive efforts back into the situation.

_____

_____

_____

_____

_____

Day Four: Encounters with the Heart of God

David, Nabal, and Abigail

Read 1 Samuel 25:2-42.

Wintertime fell, and short on supplies once again, David and his men sought a nearby wealthy landowner named Nabal. Throughout the winter months, they encamped around Nabal's flocks and herdsmen, providing protection against the wandering Bedouin tribes. David's mercenaries furnished security and built friendships with Nabal's shepherds. We can wonder if David picked this setting because he sought comfort through a familiar connection with his past. He had spent many years peacefully watching his father's sheep, and above all else at this time, David needed peace.

As springtime arrived, the fields blossomed again, fruit appeared on the vine, and the sheep-shearing season began. David sent a group of men to Nabal to ask for provisions. This was actually payment for services already rendered. The shepherds testified to their master that they had never been safer. Not one of their flocks was missing. They had been kept secure throughout the winter and springtime by David and his men. Now that it was festival time, provisions and food were plentiful. Surely David's protection had earned him a portion of the abundance.

But churlish Nabal was a fool, concerned about his own life and little else. He sent word to David that not one drop of his wine, not one piece of his fruit, nor one lamb of his flock would be given to David. Nabal insisted that he would have nothing to do with this band of renegades wandering through the Israeli outback.

David's reaction, while the opposite of the response he had with Saul, was understandable. He was angry. His men had spent the entire winter in the fields guarding Nabal's men. They had protected Nabal's herdsmen, flocks, and granaries at their own expense and risk. Now they were hungry and tired, and their own supplies were running out. Nabal had refused a simple, humble request. So David, with rage in his eyes and murder in his heart, mounted his camel. He and his men vowed that not one man of Nabal's household would remain alive by the next morning.

There is something that happens in a man's heart when he is being tested by God. He is much closer to the ground level of his emotions. He will honestly give until he has no resources left for himself, but in doing so, he sometimes will expect others to do the same. He is also camped on the edge of an emotional precipice, with little personal restraint available should that expected trust be breached. When a man is pushed beyond his human limits, God is still faithful to unearth the resources of divine supply. David's composure was gone, and in a murderous rage, he left for Nabal's home. And there, in the desert sand, he met God's divine supply…a renewal of patience and grace.

Nabal's wife, Abigail, was a wise woman. She recognized the value of David's service to their household, and she also knew the temperament of her husband. She met David with roasted lamb, figs, raisins, and skins of wine. She bowed low in the desert dust, thanked David for his sacrifice, and offered her own services to the future king.

When a man is tested by God, and the character that God hopes to build within him is breached, God is still faithful and provides a way of escape, if that man will accept it. There will always be a way to stand up under the trial, maintain integrity, and continue in the path that God has chosen for him. Sometimes that way of escape is being pulled up from failure by the hand of another. Abigail was David's escape, God's gift to him in this dangerous situation.

Not many days later, Nabal died of a stroke. At this news, David took Abigail as his own wife, and the nomadic mercenaries began to feel the gentle influence of her domestication. The presence of a wife is a civilizing influence. The possibility of children brought thoughts of a future home. Some of the men, including David, began to yearn for an end to the wilderness wanderings. The presence of David's wife and the subtle changes that she brought catalyzed a metamorphosis, turning David's heart toward home and toward the people whom he would eventually lead.

The Hills of Hakilah

Read 1 Samuel 26:1-25.

Years later, David and his men again settled in an area close to Ziph. The wilderness of Hakilah was a large domain with clumps of trees, hills, and an elevated place to camp that provided a small measure of safety. Saul again heard of David's location and mounted a final campaign to pursue David. He and his men marched south from Jerusalem for two days. That night, after troops had set up camp for the night, David and his nephew Abishai reconnoitered what could be the next day's battlefield. The biblical record tells us that God put Saul's army into a deep sleep, and David and Abishai slipped down into King Saul's camp. Lying on the ground beside the chief general was the king, asleep and vulnerable. Abishai looked at David once again. This time they weren't backed into a cave; they were standing directly above both the king and his right-hand man. With blood in his eyes, Abishai whispered, "David, let me strike him into the ground. It will only take one blow, David. This trial can be over. You have a wife now. The men are talking of having homes of their own. It is time for this to be done. God has delivered him into your hands!"

Against the tug of his own self-interest, David held true to the principles and the character that God had painstakingly built within him. He would not touch the Lord's anointed, not even if it meant wandering in this wilderness another decade. Instead, they took Saul's spear and a pot next to his head, and then scrambled off to the top of the nearest hill. From this safe distance, David called to the king, awakening him. The pot and spear were incontrovertible evidence that David had held Saul's life in his hands, and yet had spared him. In the face of David's integrity, Saul mouthed a shallow apology and then humbly retreated to Jerusalem.

Toward the end of any wilderness, you will face your own responses to God's efforts, and in those refining moments, you can catch a glimpse of God's heart. These final steps through God's desert can often lead to a temporary dead end. There may be no marked path through the outback of God's personal character-building school. When we lose our way, our failure is meant to bring us to deeper dependence on God. These three dead ends are the final obstacles you will face as you work with God in His efforts to conform your life to His image. They are:

- The boulder field of bitterness,
- The dry well of self-sufficiency, and
- The canyon of selfishness.

Responding to an unjust situation with bitterness and an unforgiving heart is a sure way to hinder God's efforts in your life. This response complicates the desert experience with two new problems. God stops working as He waits for you to deal with your unforgiveness. Only then can He continue to build your character…if you're willing to pick up on the desert trail where you left off.

When brought about by someone else's poor decisions, a desert injustice can swiftly change into a boulder-filled field of bitterness. Unforgiveness and bitterness are an easy way to pave over injustice's pain. It is a simplistic solution we use to cover hurt feelings or to find emotional momentum to tow the baggage of our wounded heart. Yet God wants to develop within us a heart that seeks after Him at all times. Will you love and offer an open hand to those who have hurt you, so they can find a reason to change? Or will you react with a closed fist, and strike back at the offender? Unforgiveness is a barrier to overcome if you find yourself in a trial of injustice.

What about you? Are there events like these that have happened in your life? Is there a current relationship which has become lodged under boulders of bitterness?

_____

_____

_____

_____

_____

_____

What have you done to this point to help or to ignore this situation?

_____

_____

_____

_____

_____

What can you now commit to do that will allow God to again begin to heal your life and the lives of others involved with you? Write your commitment in the spaces below.

_____

_____

_____

_____

_____

As you're trudging through the wilderness, the dry well of self-sufficiency may appear in the distance to seemingly offer refreshment, but it is only another manifestation of spiritual pride. When we are in the midst of a crisis, our culture has taught us to reach down deep, pull ourselves up by our own bootstraps, work harder, work longer, and become more focused on finding a solution. The wilderness of injustice is a place where God works to break your own self-sufficient habits and teach you that you are dependent on Him. This wilderness will not end until you learn to reach beyond your self-sufficiency and build friendships in the community of God's people. There we find the true strength, solace, and wisdom that we do not have in our own assets. Pride and self-sufficiency are dry wells in our desert journey, an impressive coat of paint and glossy lacquer over the dull, worn-out surfaces of our lives.

What about you? Are there actions or decisions that you have based in your own spiritual pride? Consider them closely and look for God's hand working through others to build your personal godly character.

_____

_____

_____

_____

What can you do to change this pattern of self-sufficient, arrogant behavior? What can you now commit to do that will allow God to begin again to heal your life and the lives of others involved with you? Write your commitment in the spaces below.

_____

_____

_____

_____

The canyon in the desert of preparation is one of our own selfishness. Our natural response to a difficult situation is that we become incredibly selfish. We focus on what we want — other people can wait until later. Sociologists call this a "fight-or-flight mechanism." When under stress, our natural inclination is to protect and defend ourselves against anyone who would threaten our protective shell. God may use a trial of injustice to teach us that by giving to the one who brings the injustice, by unconditionally reaching out, we can find wholeness again. We actually find healing for our own life by giving to those who created the pain. And in doing so, we personally discover new depths of God's mercy and love.

Can you see God's hand in events like these in your life?

_____

_____

What brought you into the canyon of selfishness, and how have you responded to your circumstances?

_____

_____

_____

What can you do differently — how can you now demonstrate unselfish love for others in your situation? Although these may be the hardest choices you ever make, they are the ones which will spiritually release you to grow and begin moving closer to God again.

_____

_____

_____

_____

_____

_____

Day Five: Meeting God Face to Face

During this time in David's life, God was doing a specific work and preparing David for a specific task. He was preparing David to be the king that Jews and Christians would revere for centuries. This period of preparation in David's life was the key that made his later success possible. What God formed in the wilderness was the inner man, David's character, which made his leadership over Israel, his choices of the outer man, possible.

In David's life, he wasn't given a choice as to whether or not he would submit to God's plans. God called David, and He knew what kind of man David needed to become in order to fulfill that calling. From David's perspective, to stop running would have been a death sentence at the hands of the emotionally disturbed King Saul. His course of action and the kind of life he would live during this time were not options within his control.

The only choice David had was whether he would humble himself and trust his God, or harden his heart with bitter attitudes and the question, "Why me? This isn't fair!"

That choice is the same one you and I face each time injustice enters our lives. Will you become a man or woman who, like David, does not hold on to what is rightfully yours but humbles yourself before God? Or will you insist on fulfilling your own desires, and thereby thwart what God wants to do in your life?

As you consider David, turn to what may be a familiar passage in the New Testament book of Philippians. As Christians, Paul calls you and me to foster this same attitude. Paul lived a similar life to David's, in that he suffered for the cause of the gospel. Paul looked to Jesus as his model, and he saw this same process and attitude lived by our Savior. Paul unashamedly calls you and me to take on the attitude of Christ:

> *Your attitude should be the same as that of Christ Jesus: Who, being in very nature God, did not consider equality with God something to be grasped, but made himself nothing, taking the very nature of a servant, being made in human likeness. And being found in appearance as a man, he humbled himself and became obedient to death — even death on a cross!*
>
> —Philippians 2:5-8

Jesus did not hold on to what was rightly His — a throne in heaven at His Father's right hand. He willingly came to earth as a human being in order to give His life for you and me. David did not hold on to the position which was rightfully his from the day Samuel anointed him as king. But he trusted his fate to the God who loved him, and he waited for God's supply of his needs. He did all of this with an attitude that kept his relationship with God in first place in his life.

Before going on, ask yourself: In the arena of my life, where have I placed my relationship with God? Is it absolutely in first place, given the highest priority?

_____

_____

_____

_____

How does my relationship with God affect my actions, attitudes, and beliefs?

_____

_____

_____

In what area have I kept my own hands firmly on the steering wheel of my life? My career? My family? Holding on to unforgiving attitudes and feelings toward others?

_____

_____

How could you take a step toward trusting God more completely in these areas?

_____

_____

_____

_____

We can hold on to unforgiveness so easily and justify it when the situation was unfair. But when we so strongly cling to those experiences, we are not able to open our hands and receive the blessings of a humble and meek character.

Look back over your workbook responses for this past week. Is there a dominant theme, a specific event your writing uncovered that you may need to revisit? Write your thoughts below.

_____

_____

_____

_____

_____

_____

The most important question is: What will you do with this revelation? Is there a person in your past whom you need to forgive — perhaps a parent, friend, sibling, co-worker, or ex-spouse? Releasing the hardened feelings will likely not change the offending person, but it will transform your own heart and prepare you to love again. This is part of the process to which Jesus referred when He said that "new wine cannot be poured into old wineskins" (see Matthew 9:17).

The idea of new and old wineskins was common to Jesus' listeners. Wine was poured into soft leather pouches for transport on a long journey. The chemical and fermentation action in the wine caused the leather to expand with the fermentation and then harden again as the wine was consumed. At the end of the journey, the wineskin had become a hardened shell — the leather was stiff and brittle. If new wine was again poured into the skin, the pressure of the fermentation would cause the hardened leather to crack, and then both the wine and the skin were lost. Before the old skin could be used again, it was softened by rubbing it with oil. This restored pliability to the leather and prepared it for the new wine. In the same way, our hearts must be softened and prepared for God's presence. Sometimes this preparation comes with our willingness, but at other times, God sovereignly moves to prepare us for His yet unseen purposes.

In the lines below, write your personal prayer or a list of action steps you will take to begin this process in your life. What will you do with these lessons from David's life? How will you specifically apply them to your own?

_____

_____

_____

_____

_____

_____

_____

_____

_____

_____

Father God,

When Jesus came to the earth, He not only let go of everything that was His birthright in heaven, but He lived and died for people — imperfect and ungrateful people. Lord, You knew that many, if not most, of the people for whom You gave Your life would reject You and consider Your sacrifice meaningless to their lives. When people treat me that way, and cast my best efforts aside, I often react in anger, unforgiveness, or retaliation. Lord, help me to be more like David, more like Jesus, and to become a man or woman after Your own heart. In Jesus' name I pray. Amen.

Week Three: Summary

Fearfulness and trembling are come upon me, and horror hath overwhelmed me. And I said, Oh that I had wings like a dove! for then would I fly away, and be at rest. Lo, then would I wander far off, and remain in the wilderness.... For it was not an enemy that reproached me; then I could have borne it: neither was it he that hated me that did magnify himself against me; then I would have hid myself from him. But it was thou, a man mine equal, my guide, and mine acquaintance. We took sweet counsel together, and walked unto the house of God in company.... As for me, I will call upon God; and the LORD shall save me. Evening, and morning, and at noon, will I pray, and cry aloud: and he shall hear my voice. He hath delivered my soul in peace from the battle that was against me: for there were many with me.

—Psalm 55:5-18 KJV

This week's lessons have introduced you to new ideas about David, and the way God worked in his life. What is one new idea that you have learned this week? If there is one insight or idea which God used to grab your attention, write it on the lines below.

_____

_____

_____

_____

_____

_____

_____

David

The Everyday Blast Furnace of Life

The characteristics of the kingdom emanate from the character of the king.

—Ed Cole

Day One: Take a Look at God's Word

David and his men settled into a city of their own, but after a short excursion for a military campaign, they returned to find their homes burned, and their children and wives taken by the Amalekites. After a decade of running in the wilderness and learning to lead his mercenary army, David's character had been forged by God Himself. He was being prepared for his ascension to the throne in just two short years. Like an adolescent who is moving toward adulthood, although David accepted many of the responsibilities of leading the nation, he still needed to temper his ability not only to lead, but to lead faithfully. The events at Ziklag demonstrate the proof of God's work in David's life and the blessing that you can expect when you trust God to be the Provider in your life.

Read 1 Samuel 27:1-7 and 30:1-18.

What was the city in which David and his men settled?

_____

_____

_____

How long did they live there before leaving on another military campaign?

_____

_____

_____

What happened while David and his men were away from their city?

_____

_____

_____

According to 1 Samuel 30:6, how did David respond to the situation?

_____

_____

_____

What did God tell David to do?

_____

_____

_____

What was the result?

_____

_____

_____

This week, our final week in the study of David, we will dig deeper into this account and see how David's — and our — character is often tested in the everyday blast furnaces of life.

Day Two: A Man After God's Own Heart

I joined the men gathering in the center of our village as the first glints of sunlight streamed over the distant hills. "Eliah, I want your group of fifty men to lead the column. Meet my brother Joab near the gate as we organize for today's journey."

"Jotham! Where's Jotham?" I called.

One of his groups called back, "Jotham's still in his bed, sleeping on a feather pillow." A chuckle ran through his corps. "Go, get Jotham and bring him here immediately. We cannot keep our ally waiting this morning." Surveying the men, I spotted Jacob. He had proven himself a trustworthy leader of his men. I counted on him, always in the right place at the right time as we moved toward battle.

"Jacob, I want your group to bring up the end of the column. No stragglers today. They have given us this fine city. It's no time to dishonor them by being late."

As I inspected the men, they seemed to be peaceful, even as we headed for war yet again. This morning we awakened in our own town, Ziklag. How many years had we been strewn across the countryside in hollows, caves, and oases, wondering if we would be awakened by the cries of Saul's army? But not today. Ziklag lay toward the south end of the Israelite kingdom, bordering on the Philistine's territory. They had given us this refuge at David's insistence, and because David had bartered our protection on their northern flank in order to forge the frail alliance. Joab and I had objected. "Why are we aligning ourselves with our enemies? Why are we finding sanctuary among these uncircumcised Philistines?"

David responded, "Joab and Abishai, my trusted brothers, there is a day coming when Saul will bring his army against us. These heathen, these uncircumcised Philistines may be a blessing from God's hand in that day of trouble."

What David had hoped for had come to pass. Ziklag, our own walled city, had become our haven. In the short time we had settled there, the men quickly welcomed domestic life. Joyfully I woke up each day and gazed at my wife and children. I knew that when we returned home from battle, they would be waiting here for us. Each of these men, some of whom I never thought would actually desire a family life, had begun to enjoy God's blessings brought from the unlikely hand of the uncircumcised.

When Joab and I had found David at Keilah, there had been just a handful who were faithful to him. We believed that this champion of God's people, the slayer of Goliath of Gath, deserved to have an army for his protection. As Saul's kingdom descended into disarray, Joab and I watched our own mercenary tribe grow to 600 men. A couple here, four or five there, even criminals fleeing justice from their own town found refuge with David. Some were known thieves, but David accepted each one. He seemed to be more concerned about shepherding lost sheep than returning to the fold himself.

David did require a few things from his men. First, they were to be totally honest and accountable to him. Second, each soldier was to walk as a man of integrity and honor before God, Jehovah our Provider, and to keep the laws of Israel. Third, each swore their allegiance to him, not as a king or someone to overthrow Saul, but as a shepherd who would provide for their needs. And in return they pledged him their lives.

Some of these men I still wondered about. There was grumbling and complaining among the ranks, but as Ziklag became our home, each of us looked toward heaven and thanked God for His provision through the hardships we had seen. We thanked Jehovah for this city, our new home, and for David who had earned our loyalty.

"Abishai, Abishai, how are the men this morning?" David called from his camel.

"My brother, David, the men are assembling near the gate. Joab is waiting there with Abiathar, the priest, to bless us before we leave. Where is our journey today?"

David paused. He looked refreshed, at peace. As he considered the journey, a momentary cloud of despair chased across his eyes. David struggled under the doubts that we might never return to our home. Samuel, who had anointed him to be king over a decade earlier, was now dead, and David wearied of the desert; he was the most thankful among us for the city of Ziklag. For us these walls were home; for him, they meant protection and safety for his life after a decade of running from Saul.

As fast as the expression had clouded his eyes, it was gone, and he spoke about the day's journey to the Philistine kings. "I don't know where their campaign is today," David replied, "but we will join them in the plains just north of Aphek and present ourselves there, faithfully, honoring them for the city which they have given to us."

Honoring the Philistines. The thought settled as uneasily in my belly as had last month's figs that I'd scraped from the bottom of my bag of provisions. I followed David toward the gate where we joined my brother Joab. Abiathar called for Jehovah's blessings as the men rode past. A day-and-a-half's journey would bring us to the Philistine kings on the plains of Aphek.

That night as we encamped in a half-green oasis, David walked among the men's campfires. He was not one to stay in his tent. Jacob's wife had just birthed his first son. Jotham's brother had just rebuilt the roof and strengthened the gate on his house. Each one had his own story to tell — their new concerns back in the village — and David listened tirelessly. He consistently directed their attention to Jehovah God for His provision and personally thanked them with his presence among them.

After the fires died and the men slept for the night, I walked by David's tent on the way to my own. I heard him singing the song I knew he had written as a boy:

> *"The Lord is my Shepherd, and I shall not want.*
> *He leads me to lie down in green pastures.*
> *He anoints my head and my cup overflows.*
> *He prepares a table before me in the presence of my enemies.*
> *Surely goodness and mercy shall follow me all the days of my life*
> *And I shall dwell in the house of the Lord forever and ever."*

I revered this man who had guided our lives, and I was beginning to understand the deep well from which he drew his strength. It wasn't in the strength of our troops, their skill, or their numbers. Even in the midst of the difficulties we encountered, David truly was a man pursuing God, not war, and I wished I could have a piece of his faith for my own.

In the morning, David, Joab, and I led the column of men onto the wind-swept plains of Aphek. Our men stayed a respectful distance behind, while Joab and I continued toward the lords of the Philistines. David motioned Joab and me to stop as he joined King Achish. They talked under colorful tribal flags that snapped in the breeze. Animated speech drifted over the plains, punctuated with flailing arms and shouts of disagreement from the other lords. Then, in a strange move, Achish motioned to each of his commanders and asked them a quiet question. Each shook their heads no. Were we to lose our city? The intensity of my fears caught me off guard. Although we had called Ziklag our home for only a short time, the village had come to represent more than just my bed and cottage. It meant security and safety after years of struggle. But as I watched David speak with the princes of the Philistines and their king, I took solace in his faith in God. Finding strength as I looked to heaven, I discovered the faith that David exhibited every day.

"Abishai, Joab, we have been given leave today to return to our homes. The Israelites are camped in Jezreel, and the Philistines are going to war against them. Jehovah has blessed us, for how could we fight against our brothers? The Lord has watched over us again. Against Israel, with our army on their flank, they feared we would turn against them. That was a risk they weren't willing to take."

His words brought peace to my soul. With joy I returned to the men and announced, "We're returning home, brothers. We've been given relief from today's battle. Let's return home to our families, our houses, our flocks, and our children. There we can rest in the plenty that God has given us."

Until that moment I hadn't realized how fatigued we had become with war. Each man stood stalwart and true, with his sword and shield at his side, ready to follow David's lead. With the reprieve, joy rippled across the men like the spring tides on the Galilean shore. They talked of their wives, children, and homes. Although we had grown accustomed to the trial of war, it was a weight we gladly left in the desert sun this day. Each man turned in formation with Eliah at the lead and Jacob taking up the rear, heading for home.

Camp was pitched in the same green valley as the previous night, and as the fires dotted the hillside among the trees, the air was filled with joy and laughter. Jacob talked about holding his newborn son. Joab spoke with other captains, remembering the victories Jehovah had given them, and the friends they had lost in battle. Joab prayerfully acknowledged the God who had provided relief when they needed it most. As David walked among the men again, he bore each man's respect. His confidence in Jehovah went before him, yet the humility with which he led our community was never farther away than his shadow. He sat with Jacob and asked him about his wife, his daughter, and his new son. He spoke with the men who had elderly parents. David knew the tribe each called his family: the Benjaminites, Judah's sons, and the Reubenites. His genuine interest for all of us as his brothers had built these mercenaries into a community that could be trusted, the men to whom David had pledged his protection and his life. Again, I heard him singing as I passed his tent late in the evening — psalms of joy and peace as he spent the evening watch before Jehovah Jireh, our Provider.

The morning came early. Every man was eager to get home. Even Jotham was out of bed on time. His tent was down, and his men were in formation before the sun danced in the treetops. The men talked and laughed on this last leg of the journey, at times running ahead of the camels.

We crested the hill which bordered Ziklag, and the column came to an abrupt halt. The joy and laughter fell silent at the head of the ranks, and David called for Joab and me to join him. As we stepped into the pass and looked down into the valley, my soul collapsed.

Ziklag lay ransacked and burned. The gates were gone, as were all signs of life from our homes. There were no children in the courtyard, no flocks outside the gates, no women moving through the marketplace. The acrid smell of burnt timber and scorched desert sand drifted out of the valley and turned our joy into mourning. As the whispers began, I heard an anguished cry from the very back. Jacob was weeping for his daughter, his newborn son, and his wife. What had happened?

The entire battalion pressed into the pass overlooking our city. Smoke still rose from some of the homes. Soon we were all on our knees, and then our faces, before God, throwing dust in the air, wondering what we had done to bring His judgment down upon us. Our moments of joy had suddenly been replaced by sorrow as deep as any I had ever experienced.

We wept for our children and our homes. But the deep anguish welling from my soul was for the fragile security that had been ripped from my heart. Hope deferred! My heart lay shattered before my brothers and my God. We wept until we had strength to weep no more. And then, just as quickly as joy had been replaced by sorrow, it rolled away under ominous clouds of confusion — and anger. Murmuring started against the One who had been our protection from heaven, and grumbling against the one who had been our leader through the desert.

"We should never have left our homes in the first place," one man said.

"Who is this David, that we should trust him?" grumbled another.

"I knew that making an alliance with the Philistines was a sin against Jehovah!" retorted a third. "This is God's hand of punishment for our disobedience, for trusting in the uncircumcised."

The men whom David had protected for years suddenly crystallized into an angry mob, and David stood precariously at the vortex of their anger. But he was still on his face before God. He was still weeping. He refused to get up, even at the urging of my brother Joab.

"David," said Joab, "the men need you! David, what are we to do?"

With his head still bowed low, David was yet unscorched by the garrison's rising temperature. But their anger, like the flames that had consumed our homes, was ready to turn on David and extinguish his frail life. From the back I heard Jacob call out, "Someone hand me a rock! I'll end this would-be king's reign. It is time for us to return home, to our real homes!"

Scuffling for position, these 600 battle-hardened warriors teetered dangerously on the edge of civil war. Accusations erupted; some pushed for position while others reached for rocks, their shields, or their swords. Those of us who supported David feared for his life, and our own. Joab and I wheeled instinctively, placing ourselves between David and the rising tumult. I turned to protect my brother Joab, and felt his back press hard against mine. We had slain many soldiers from this combat stance under the desert sun, but never our own brothers. Above the clamor, I heard Joab unsheath his sword. As I reached for my own, a shadow fell across my feet. The clamor abated; it was not peace, but a temporary reprieve as if we had passed into the eye of a storm. I turned to see David standing on a large rock, overlooking the angry throng. His stature wordlessly commanded our attention.

David had been here before…running from Saul in the middle of the night, hiding in the caves of En Gedi. David knew the loss of everything he held precious. He had learned to take mourning and brokenness into Jehovah's presence, and wait there for renewed strength. David's face was stained red and brown from tears and dirt. The moisture from his nose clung to the corners of his mouth and stained the front of his tunic. Having poured out his entire heart, soul, and strength before God, his face wore not only his own pain, but his pain and sorrow for his men. In all this, his tattered appearance failed to overshadow the stature of the man he had become.

"We will track them down," David called out. His voice cracked from weeping, but every man heard his confidence. "We will pursue them! We will find our families. We will find our children. We will find our flocks, and we will return them to our homes!"

I mounted my camel to the sound of rocks being returned to their rightful place on the hot desert floor. Each man found his sword in the sand, and fell into rank behind his captain. I turned to Joab, and said quietly, "I will follow this man to my last breath!"

David faced one of the most difficult challenges of early leadership. His men, and those whom he had been charged to protect, turned on him. His personal performance of the last years meant nothing in this moment. The pertinent question was whether or not David had learned the character and confidence to stand and wait on his God to encourage and lead him during times of trouble. God promises victory, but not necessarily external peace. When we are faced with trials, tribulations, temptations, or injustice, the only relevant question becomes, Will we throw in the towel, and give in to our own fears, or will we continue to pursue God in order to reach the victory He promises? When we choose the latter, we prove that we are becoming a vessel fit for the Master's use, a man or woman after His own heart.

Principle four in the process God uses to mold and change our hearts is this:

Principle Four: Adolescent leaders, regardless of their age, are tested before they are released. The choices they make define and refine their godly character in the blast furnace of life.

How would you have responded to this situation if you had been in David's shoes?

_____

_____

_____

_____

If you had been one of the men following him?

_____

_____

_____

Record any thoughts or insights you have gained from the study of this trial in David's life.

_____

_____

_____

_____

_____

_____

_____

_____

_____

_____

Day Three: Walking in David's Footsteps

David's life was transformed by God during his wilderness trials. He learned God's provision. He learned to trust in Jehovah-Jireh, his Provider, and not to take events into his own hands. He discovered firsthand that God is the One who brings success and triumph in every area of life, that his victories were not his own. But before he was released to lead God's people, David went through a final test, one in which he was forced to apply these lessons to the choices that he faced in life. David had an opportunity to take Saul's life, and he didn't. At Ziklag, David had the opportunity to quit, and he refused. Instead, David fell on his face and encouraged himself in the Lord. Then he arose to pursue God and pursue the things that God had promised him.

David could have justified his loss, surrendered to the trials he faced, and said to himself, *What I really wanted must not have been God's plan for me. It must have been my own ideas.* But despair's subtle temptation lost its pull on David's heart as he applied the lessons he had learned in the desert and waited on God in prayer. He stayed firm in the Lord through the unfair and difficult trials, even when his own men lost faith in him. He waited on the Lord and found the strength to continue because of the man he had become. The young leader was tempered in the blast furnace. He was molded into the man we later see on the throne of Israel, leading God's people, a man after God's own heart.

A time that tests the lessons you have learned will often follow your experiences of living through difficult times. I call this period of time, "testing adolescent leadership in the blast furnace of everyday life."

What about you? Have there been troubling events in your life that, from your vantage point now, you can see were God's way of testing your heart? Maybe lessons you learned as a young believer are now being put to the test, and you have a new opportunity to choose to live them out. What specific events from your life come to mind as we look at this final event in David's life? Write your thoughts below.

_____

_____

_____

_____

_____

_____

_____

What were the results of some of the trials you have gone through and lessons you have learned in your Christian life?

_____

_____

_____

_____

_____

_____

What did you do to encourage yourself in the Lord and stay faithful in a situation that tried your faith?

_____

_____

_____

_____

What can you do now to make new choices and live out the things you have learned? Write your thoughts below.

_____

_____

_____

_____

_____

_____

_____

Day Four: Out of the Furnace and into Real Life

Many Old Testament writers used the picture of a furnace when describing the process God uses to prepare His people. This process is not reserved for just kings and leaders, because God wishes to create a pure heart in every one of His children. Malachi said that God is like a refiner's fire, purifying His children as gold. Zechariah wrote in one of his messianic prophecies that God will bring His people through the fire so that they will say, "The Lord is my God." Isaiah wrote that God will turn His hand on His people and purge away their impurities in order to create or restore a relationship with Him.

Read the following scriptures, and record specific thoughts about how God may be applying this to your life right now. Prayerfully consider specific areas of your life that need God's purifying fire to draw you closer to Him.

Malachi 3:1-4

_____

_____

Zechariah 13:6-9

_____

_____

Isaiah 1:18-26

_____

_____

While in our modern day we have developed steel smelting plants to create usable metals from mined ore, the skillful process of purifying metal ore was more personally familiar to those who lived in David's time. When metal ore was taken from the ground, the impurities rendered it dull, brittle, and less useful than pure metals. So the refiner would put a chunk of ore into his ceramic refining bowl and place the bowl over a strong fire.

As the metal coalesced, impurities rose to the top of the bowl, and the pure metal settled in the bottom. The refiner would then pour off the impurities, leaving pure iron, silver, or gold in his bowl.

As refiners compared their efforts, they discovered that some of the metals were harder, shinier, or more useful than others. By experimenting with different temperatures, the refiners discovered that different impurities rose to the surface when the heat temperature was varied. So the refining process turned into a series of heating, pouring off the impurities, or dross, and repeating the process to achieve a pure metal, ready for use in whatever way was needed.

Take a few minutes and review the scriptures listed above. What can you see about how God used this process during David's sojourn in the wilderness?

_____

_____

_____

What can you see that may be part of God's purifying purposes in your own life?

_____

_____

_____

The apostle Paul's life was filled with trials. Between the victorious times of healing the sick and spreading the gospel, he was thrown in prison, beaten, and otherwise persecuted for preaching the gospel. On his journey to Rome as a prisoner, he was shipwrecked, marooned on an island, and then bitten by a snake! At the end of his life, he shared about this purifying process with his dear friend Timothy. From his jail cell in Rome, Paul wrote his final letter, and had this to say:

> _In a large house there are articles not only of gold and silver, but also of wood and clay; some are for noble purposes and some for ignoble. If a man cleanses himself from the latter, he will be an instrument for noble purposes, made holy, useful to the Master and prepared to do any good work._
>
> —2 Timothy 2:20-21

Directly before this commission to Timothy to keep his life pure, Paul identified those things that would corrupt a man's life, and from verse 22 through the end of the chapter, Paul encouraged Timothy to foster the kind of traits that would bring about God's purposes in his life.

Read 2 Timothy 2:14-26, and write below the specific instructions for "becoming a vessel fit for the Master's use."

_____

_____

What are the "ignoble" and common influences, which keep your life from being used for God's purposes?

_____

_____

What are the "noble" purposes, signs of a consecrated life ready for God's work to be done?

_____

_____

_____

_____

How can you apply this to your life and heart in order to become more like Christ and demonstrate the heart of God to your world?

_____

_____

_____

_____

_____

_____

_____

_____

Day Five: Lessons from David's Life

For the past four weeks we have considered four snapshots of David's life: his anointing by Samuel, his friendship with Jonathan and flight from Saul, his life in the wilderness, and the ransacking of his home village, Ziklag.

These events outline a process that God uses for the express purpose of forging godly character, for changing our hearts from a self-centered perspective to a God-centered one. Let's review these four principles.

Principle One

We meet God, begin a personal relationship with Him, and receive a personal revelation of His love for us.

Principle Two

God provides the opportunity for a period of initial peace, victory, or success, but then He shapes our lives through circumstances, events, or other people. This time can include both unexpected blessing and unjust trials.

Principle Three

God's loving tests continue until we come to a place of utter dependence on Him. We learn to look to Him and behave in ways consistent with God's character, regardless of whatever injustice, trial, or opportunity for temporary personal gain comes our way.

Principle Four

Adolescent leaders, regardless of their age, are tested before they are released. The choices they make define and refine their godly character in the blast furnace of life.

David progressed from an outcast adolescent, into a steeled yet tenderhearted man after God's own heart. He then matured further into a man whom God could trust to lead His people.

Take a minute and mentally leaf through the pages of your life. If you were to place yourself in this process, where would you find yourself today? Write your insights below.

_____

_____

_____

What things can you do to participate with God, and move on to the next principle? What things must be left up to God?

_____

_____

_____

In what other ways can you apply these lessons from David's life into your own? Take a few minutes, review your notes from the previous weeks, and write specific steps you can take that will further God's purposes in your life.

_____

_____

_____

_____

_____

_____

There is often a pattern in your life that remains hidden until you gaze into the mirror of God's Word. God's ultimate purpose is that you, your character, and your personality become more and more like His. God's ultimate will is that you take on His own divine character. The pattern to which you will conform will spring from the lessons you are learning, or how you resist the changes God desires to bring into your life.

Look through your journal entries in the last four chapters. At the end of each chapter, you have recorded a dominant lesson that was meaningful to you. Take the time to review your notes, and in the lines below, record any major theme you have expressed over the past four weeks. God works in the stillness of our hearts, and in the personal honesty of your journal you are likely to see His fingerprints.

What do you believe God would want you to do with these insights you have gained?

_____

_____

Commit your personal application of these lessons to God in a prayer, as we complete this section of our study.

> *Father God,*
>
> *You stood with David when he could not see the reasons for the struggles in his life. You were his Shield, his Tower, and the One to whom he ran when he had no one else to turn to. Father, in my own life, I avoid facing injustice, and I recoil from difficulty or suffering of any kind. Yet, You used these very tools to mold David's life into one that fulfilled Your purposes, and his heart into a heart which beat with Yours.*
>
> *Father, I want to be like David, and even more, like Christ. Transform my character and heart so that I can follow You and fulfill Your purposes in my world. Help me find the courage to participate with You, and do those things that You require of me.*
>
> *In Jesus' name. Amen.*

Week Four: Summary

Even the youths shall faint and be weary, and the young men shall utterly fall:
But they that wait upon the LORD shall renew their strength; they shall mount up
with wings as eagles; they shall run, and not be weary; and they shall walk, and
not faint.

—Isaiah 40:30-31 KJV

This lesson has completed our study of David, and the way God worked in his life. If there is one insight or idea which summarizes what you have learned so far, write it on the lines below.

_____

_____

_____

_____

_____

_____

_____

_____

_____

_____

_____

_____

Now we will go back in time several hundred years and turn to the life of another important figure in the history of the nation of Israel: Joseph, the prince of Egypt.

SECTION TWO
Joseph

Introduction to Section Two

The account of Joseph and his rise to fame is one of the most well-known beloved stories in the Old Testament. Sold by his brothers into slavery, Joseph endured years of injustice, misunderstanding, and slave labor, to eventually rise to the second most powerful man in Egypt. How was God able to take this young boy and transform him into a man who would rule the earth's most powerful nation? The Bible leaves out so many details about his father, Jacob, and his eleven brothers. What were they like? What kind of culture existed in Jacob's home?

But the most important details are given that tell us what we need to know about Joseph's life: Without Joseph there would have been no need for Moses. Without Joseph there would have been no Ten Commandments, Passover, covenant at Mt. Sinai — or Christ. Joseph's perseverance and eventual triumph teach us many things about pursuing the character — and the heart — of God.

How did God choose this young man? And more importantly, what did God do to prepare him for his role of expanded influence and leadership? The answers to these questions will further illustrate the process God uses to change your heart as you seek Him and seek to become someone who "serves God's purposes in your generation."

Joseph

A Cry in the Wilderness

*You cannot control all the details
or the length of your life,
but you can have something
to say about its width and depth.*

Day One: Take a Look at God's Word

Joseph was born into a family rich with heritage and full of promise. Jacob, Joseph's father, was one of Isaac's two sons, and a grandson of Abraham. Although this family had been chosen from among all peoples of the earth and set apart for God's special purpose, God's plan did not prevent Jacob from growing up as a manipulative conniver. Jacob learned how to get what he wanted through deceit. He learned early in his life how to take advantage of others' weaknesses, and he used these skills to rob his brother, Esau, of his birthright. Yet God chose Jacob's lineage to eventually bring the Savior into the world. The genealogy of Jesus can be traced back through King David, to Abraham, Isaac — and Jacob.

We have the advantage of being able to read the final pages of the story in Scripture, but Jacob did not have that convenience. He suffered through difficult circumstances and divinely orchestrated events, and eventually became the father of Israel. The beginnings of Jacob's — and Joseph's — story is found in Genesis 29 through 35.

Take the time today to read each of these chapters. Record below the major themes in each passage, as well as a lesson you can take away.

Chapter 29: Jacob's Family

_____

_____

_____

_____

_____

Chapter 30: Jacob's Sons

_____

_____

_____

_____

_____

Chapter 31: Jacob Establishes His Own Home

_____

_____

_____

_____

_____

Chapter 32: Jacob Wrestles with His Brother, and His God

_____

_____

_____

_____

_____

Chapter 33: Jacob's Response to God's Blessing

_____

_____

_____

_____

_____

Chapter 34: Dinah's Rape and Jacob's Sons' Response

_____

_____

_____

_____

_____

Chapter 35: The Birth of Jacob's Youngest Son, and Rachel's Death

_____

_____

_____

_____

Day Two: Jacob's Divided Home

A Desert Family

The Bible tells us that when Jacob left his father's house in search of a bride, he encountered and immediately fell in love with Rachel. Her father and his uncle, Laban, asked that Jacob dedicate seven years of labor in exchange for Rachel's betrothal. Those seven years passed as a single day for Jacob, but at the end of the allotted time, Jacob was deceived into marrying Leah, Rachel's older sister. When Jacob protested, Laban gave a rather flimsy excuse: It was not proper for him to give away his younger daughter before the eldest was married first. But he would "keep his promise" with Jacob — under a new arrangement of an additional seven years' labor. The consequences of Laban's demands and Jacob's decision to marry the two sisters would affect Jacob's life and offspring for generations to come.

Soon after their marriage, it became clear that Rachel, Jacob's beloved, was barren. Leah, the older sister, saw the love that flowed from Jacob to her younger sister, but she experienced none of this love personally. But unlike Rachel, Leah was fertile, and she began producing children immediately. This cruel twist only exacerbated the rivalry between the sisters. Leah's anguish and animosity for her sister are forever recorded in the names she gave to her first two sons. Reuben, her firstborn and Jacob's first son, was named so because "God saw my misery." Simeon arrived next and received his name because Leah "was not loved." The third son was called Levi because of Leah's hope that "at last Jacob will love me." Finally, Judah arrived, and Leah proclaimed, "At last I will praise God." She expected peace now that she had produced a stalwart family of young men. Certainly Jacob would finally turn his attention to her, even as her barren sister still struggled with the embarrassment of childlessness.

Not to be outdone, however, Rachel reacted by giving Jacob her handmaiden, Bilhah. This practice was common in that culture — the sons conceived through the union of a woman's handmaiden and her husband would be considered her own. The Bible recounts Sarah and Abraham's walking down the same arduous path while waiting for their promised son, Isaac. Jacob undoubtedly knew the story. His grandfather, Abraham, was alive for the first fourteen years of Jacob's life, and the conflict between Isaac and Ishmael was already shaping the tribes' futures.

Jacob should have learned from his grandfather's error. The strife that existed between Isaac and his half-brother, Ishmael, was recent history to Jacob (and it still goes on to this day!). Nevertheless, Jacob slept with Bilhah and conceived Dan, whose name, given by Rachel, meant, "Now I have been vindicated." Next came Naphtali, Jacob's sixth son and, through Bilhah, Rachel's second. By selecting his name, Rachel said, "I have won a great struggle with my sister."

Not to be outsmarted, Leah offered her handmaiden, Zilpah, to Jacob. Gad and Asher were born from this union and Leah cried, "I am now happy with my family." Their names reflected her desires for the future and her perceived triumph over her younger childless sister.

The contest to secure Jacob's love continued for decades. Son number nine, Issachar, was conceived when Leah actually "hired" Jacob to sleep with her — to have her husband for a night, Leah paid Rachel a fee of a handful of mandrakes, desert flowers that were considered to be a "love medicine" at that time. Then came Zebulun, Jacob's tenth son. His name reflects Leah's still unmet desire: "Now my husband will treat me with honor."

These ten children, despite the nature of their conception and birth, were a part of God's plan to usher salvation into the world. Although it was full of contention and strife, God Himself had designed this community, and into Jacob's very family life He would reveal the pattern for the salvation of His people.

The Desert Life

Our modern term *dysfunctional* could have been invented by Jacob and his family! Jacob had wrestled with his older brother, Esau, and cheated him out of his birthright. He wrestled with God to receive a blessing. He wrangled Laban out of his best flocks — and both of his daughters. And now his family wrestled each other for his love and affection. These distorted relationships constituted Jacob's understanding of "normal." His life had been filled with unhealthy personal relationships since the time he and his brother, Esau, first competed for their father's blessings. But now as his family began to grow, Jacob was oblivious to the personal tragedies that were taking place — the fallout of the choices he and the others in his family had made.

Through all of this, Jacob and Rachel still longed for a son of their own, from their own union. After falling in love with Rachel, Jacob had spent fourteen years in service to Laban to marry her. Twenty-five years or more had passed, and ten sons and a daughter had been added to his clan — but none from his beloved.

Jacob's other sons were growing and were beginning to take their place in the community. On the backside of the desert, an extended family created such a community and provided increased security and safety for each other. Barren life on the desert plains required hard work to conquer the adversarial terrain, but as the proverb goes, many hands make light work, and the contribution of Jacob's older sons had earned them a well-deserved position of recognition in the family. As seasons rolled into years, the older sons undoubtedly became the backbone of the family's strength. They put up tents and worked alongside Jacob in the planting season and harvest time. By the time the ninth and tenth sons arrived, it is quite likely that the oldest group, Reuben, Simeon, Levi, and Judah, were building their own families, raising their own children, and transforming Jacob's small family into a thriving community — led by two quarrelsome wives, four birthmothers, and a father who was oblivious to most of the rancor. And yet Jacob and Rachel longed for a child to call their own.

While the time span between Reuben's birth and Joseph's arrival is not specified, we can gauge Joseph's arrival by an event that took place when Joseph was still a child. In Genesis 34, one of Jacob's daughters was abducted and raped by Shechem, a member of a nearby tribe. Afterward, Shechem felt he had fallen in love with the girl and wanted to marry her, but Jacob's outraged sons took matters into their own hands. They went to Shechem's tribe directly and said, "You may have our sister's hand in marriage, but first you must be circumcised like we are." On the third day, while the men were still in pain from their circumcisions, Simeon and Levi fell upon the town and slew every man, retrieving their sister along with the tribe's flocks and wealth.

Had Simeon and Levi been young boys, they could not have risen against this neighboring tribal community. They would not have possessed the strength and prowess necessary, nor would they have had the desire to avenge their sister's rape. Their temperament is that of young men in their twenties or early thirties, warriors who defended their father's house and their family's honor. Reuben, Simeon, and Levi were much older than Joseph; they had toiled for years as faithful sons, but with the arrival of their younger brother, everything changed.

Jacob's heartfelt cry for a son by Rachel was finally fulfilled, and it was clear to all that Jacob's new favor now rested on this child. The years of toil the older sons had invested with their father now lay abandoned, trampled in the desert dust. Whatever attention their father had given their mother, Leah, now turned, solely and completely, to Rachel. As they tended sheep in the fields and watched their baby brother grow, the typical envious feelings that most older siblings have toward the youngest were amplified by the biased treatment that seemed to show the nature of this family.

Against this backdrop, the story of Joseph's tumultuous life begins. Joseph came to his brothers one afternoon, wearing his multi-colored coat. The brightly woven robe had been Jacob's sign to everyone in the family of his favoritism — and that he intended Joseph to be his heir. Adding insult to injury, Joseph's youthful arrogance led him to pronounce his dreams of grandeur to his brothers. This proved to be an almost fatal mistake, and it was to forever alter Joseph's life.

Let's read what happened:

And when they saw him afar off, even before he came near unto them, they conspired against him to slay him. And they said one to another, Behold, this dreamer cometh. Come now therefore, and let us slay him, and cast him into some pit, and we will say, Some evil beast hath devoured him: and we shall see what will become of his dreams. And Reuben heard it, and he delivered him out of their hands; and said, Let us not kill him. And Reuben said unto them, Shed no blood, but cast him into this pit that is in the wilderness, and lay no hand upon him; that he might rid him out of their hands, to deliver him to his father again. And it came to pass, when Joseph was come unto his brethren, that they stript Joseph out of his coat, his coat of many colours that was on him; And they took him, and cast him into a pit: and the pit was empty, there was no water in it. And they sat down to eat bread: and they lifted up their eyes and looked, and, behold, a company of Ishmeelites came from Gilead with their camels bearing spicery and balm and myrrh, going to carry it down to Egypt. And Judah said unto his brethren, What profit is it if we slay our

brother, and conceal his blood? Come, and let us sell him to the Ishmeelites, and
let not our hand be upon him; for he is our brother and our flesh. And his brethren
were content. Then there passed by Midianites merchantmen; and they drew and
lifted up Joseph out of the pit, and sold Joseph to the Ishmeelites for twenty pieces of
silver: and they brought Joseph into Egypt.

—Genesis 37:18-28 KJV

Consider the similarities between what we've already studied in David's life and what would be the next twenty years in Joseph's journey. After David had become the warrior champion of Israel, he was then unjustly persecuted by Saul. Joseph's life descended from that of a privileged, favored son to a slave — in a matter of hours. Whether or not he would have clothes or another meal, where he would sleep, and what tasks he would perform, were all in the hands of those whom he would learn to call "master." His life was no longer his own, just as David experienced. The substance of their very lives had been taken out of their own control.

Consider what you have learned about the circumstances of Joseph's life. What are your thoughts about Jacob's family?

_____

_____

_____

How would you have felt and acted if you had been in Joseph's shoes?

_____

_____

_____

What do you think about the similarities between Joseph and David during this time in their lives? What similarities can you see, and how did these circumstances affect the lives, consciences, and character of these young men?

_____

_____

_____

_____

_____

Day Three: The Road to Egypt

Shackled to camels in the traders' caravan, Joseph shuffled through the sands until they reached Egypt's capital city. His wrists were chafed from the rope that secured his arms behind his back. Long ago he had stopped trying to spit the gritty sand out of his mouth. His lips cracked under the merciless sun, and his keeper's rations of bread and water had been barely enough to keep him alive for the three-week journey

As the traders entered the golden city, Joseph gawked at the gilded buildings and huge pyramids. He'd never seen anything like them before. Egypt, with its rich Nile delta and placement at the southeast corner of the Great Sea, was quickly becoming the world center of commerce. As Joseph surveyed the surreal wealth of this bustling metropolis, his own stomach growled and brought him back to harsh slave realities.

The marketeers' carts overflowed with brightly colored fruits, melons, and flowers. But Joseph had eaten nothing but bread and water during the journey. The last pleasant memory Joseph could conjure was of himself just days before, a scrawny, arrogant teenager, dressed in a multicolored coat and standing on a rock in the pasture. He remembered declaring his dreams to his brothers, and how they, his father, and his mother all bowed down to him. Now Joseph was on the auction block in the Egyptian market. He would make no proclamations today.

As Joseph stood on the block, his Ishmaelite captor snapped his back with a camel's lash. A stooped and frail-looking slave brought little profit. Joseph involuntarily pulled himself to full stature. His stalwart youthful frame caught the hungry crowd's attention. They eyed him and called to the auctioneer in languages Joseph had never heard. Who held his fate now? Joseph watched the other slaves as they were auctioned before him. Some were led away by kindly merchants, and others were yanked off the platform by their hair. His only sense of what his future held was that it would be an existence he could not comprehend.

Someone once said that faith is coming to the end of the light and taking one more step. Faith is coming to the end of what you know, but because of your trust in God, finding the courage to go on with no assurance of the outcome. Joseph had lived in the secure limelight of his parents' love. Now life had abruptly shoved him into the darkness…into a journey that would span the next twenty-plus years of his life. As he stood on the auction block, he was no longer the pampered favorite child. His head was full of doubts, his stomach was full of hunger, and he had absolutely nothing to call his own.

What had gotten him here? Dreams…crazy, stupid dreams. He was certain at the time that his dreams had been divine, that they had meant something…but now those dreams were more responsible for dragging him to this desolate Egyptian marketplace than the Ishmaelites' caravan.

My brothers bowing down to me? How could I have been so proud? My mother, father…the moon and the sun also bowing down? How could I have been so arrogant?

This was Joseph's time to despair. He had every right to surrender to the doubts and fears that filled his soul. Yet, like David, another castaway leader-in-training, Joseph knew that there was a father back home who still loved him. David's "father back home" was his heavenly Father, whose love he had experienced while watching the sheep and singing psalms. David had lived a castaway life in his own family, but he found love in the protective hands of his good Shepherd. Joseph had learned love from his earthly father, who would have given him anything. And at that moment, as Joseph looked down the dark tunnel of his future, the only visible light was his father's continuing love, and the character that love had forged into his young life. That love would sustain Joseph throughout his ordeal. The love and respect Jacob had shown him — as well as the strength he gleaned from his heavenly Father — would give him the courage to be a man of honor and integrity in the face of despair and injustice.

There are few events in life that have the power to change the course of your life forever. Hope can give you reason to look for positive progress in the face of immeasurable despair. Faith can give you the reason to choose to act in ways that contradict your circumstances. And love, built into your heart through acts of others — including God — will give you the knowledge that you are of value, and that you can face whatever life brings across your path.

And this leads us to the next principle in the process that God uses to mold our hearts and characters:

Principle Five: We find the courage and personal strength to remain faithful to our beliefs because of positive mentoring relationships in our life. As a child, or as an adult, mentoring relationships are necessary to change our heart and mold our character into a vessel that God can use.

Consider the mentors you have had in your life. How have they helped you to grow in your spiritual walk? How have they strengthened you in difficult times?

_____

_____

_____

To whom could you be a mentor yourself? In what ways could you strengthen and encourage others on the path God has chosen for them?

_____

_____

_____

_____

Day Four: Joseph, David, and the Value of Mentoring

The similarities between David and Joseph's lives are striking. They both rose to positions of early prominence only to be dumped — as if from the back of a garbage truck — into unjust and difficult situations. Yet they both stayed true to God's calling and purposes in the midst of these difficult circumstances.

Pause for a moment and consider the decisions that Joseph would have faced on a daily basis. Would he remain true to God and cultivate hope, even when despair could have engulfed him?

What do you think his motivation was for remaining faithful to God?

_____

_____

From what strength did Joseph draw in order to repeatedly earn the respect of his overlords?

_____

_____

_____

Consider Joseph the slave. His life was one of no thanks, no gratitude or recognition. He labored with no control over his future. From his perspective, why not grudgingly do his work and no more? Joseph had no guarantee, tangible or even remote, that his life would ever change. Why did he consistently outperform his peers — going above and beyond the call of duty?

What do you think?

_____

_____

_____

_____

Have you ever been in a similar circumstance? Literal slavery has been outlawed for centuries, but it's still possible to feel like a slave, stuck in a dead-end situation, under the control of others, with no hope of ever finding your way out.

Have you ever experienced this kind of environment?

_____

_____

What are the motivations that pull at your heart when you face a difficult trial? You can find strength from many sources. Anger is a powerful motivator. Self-righteousness can compel you to act, and unforgiveness carries a huge amount of emotional momentum.

But these emotional propellants lead to bitterness, and a bitter attitude is a lethal poison that slowly kills God's life within you. Joseph demonstrated his faithfulness to principles higher than the circumstances that surrounded him, and God was free to continue His work in Joseph's life.

Think again about the events you described above. What were your responses? Were you able to change the circumstances on your own? What happened that eventually changed the circumstances, or are you still engrossed in them? If the situation is ongoing, what do you think God would want you to do in order to release Him to work?

_____

_____

_____

_____

_____

_____

_____

After finally rising to a place of respect and responsibility despite his circumstances, Joseph was _again_ unjustly accused and imprisoned for something that he had not done. Why not give in now? All of his efforts seemed to be for nothing. Joseph went from a place of responsibility managing the captain of the guard's home, to a hole in the ground. He now lived his life among the dying. Yet he still held on to hope. What was it that empowered him? The answer is simple. Somewhere in Joseph's life he had experienced a relationship with a loving mentor who had built the image of faithfulness and integrity into his soul. Jacob's love for his son had imprinted indelibly on Joseph's soul that Joseph had personal worth. Joseph's life mattered to Jacob, and Joseph had learned that his life was important, regardless of the circumstances in which he found himself. So during his trials, Joseph's life was anchored to a reason to remain faithful. He chose, day by day, to look toward the heavens and say, "Somewhere there is a God who loves me. Somewhere there is a family who gave my life meaning. And to that meaning I will be true."

You may or may not have had the blessing of this kind of family. But if you're walking in God's kingdom today, at some point in time, God called you to Himself, and you discovered a different lifestyle than that of the world around you.

Take a moment and describe the person who has made the most positive impact on your life.

_____

_____

_____

_____

_____

Are there characteristics, beliefs, or personality traits in your own life that have come about as a result of that mentoring relationship? Are there things you believe, you enjoy, or are important to you that you can now see came from that mentor's influence?

_____

_____

_____

_____

_____

_____

_____

_____

_____

_____

_____

Day Five: Changing from the Inside Out

In the personal revelation of love that comes into your life from God or a unique individual such as a mentor, you can find the strength to faithfully endure difficult times. Every life has its times of trial. In our success-driven culture, we often try to avoid them. We plan for our lives to minimize the distractions and attempt to immunize ourselves against failure. But God's Word plainly says that difficulty and trials are part of every Christian's experience.

Look up the following verses and summarize what they have to say about the Christian life.

1 Peter 1:6-8

_____

_____

_____

1 Peter 4:12-13

_____

_____

_____

James 1:2-4

_____

_____

_____

When troubles come, not *if* they come, the question to consider is, how will you respond? Will you take hold of the promises and the revelation of God's character and make them a part of your life, or will you run and hide? Will you run to other people for comfort, or will you find a quiet corner in which to sulk and wait for the trial to pass? Will you argue and complain to God about what He is doing in your life? Or, as Joseph did, will you continue to show God's character through the choices that you make?

Think about difficult times that you have experienced in your life. What is the significant trial or unjust situation that comes first to your mind? Describe it below.

_____

_____

_____

_____

_____

What has been your response to this event?

_____

_____

_____

_____

Looking back at the trial and your response to it, what were the results? Did you see God's hand moving within the circumstances? Or did you sow your own selfish actions and respond out of your own carnal desires, only to reap a harvest of the same?

_____

_____

_____

_____

When the event you are considering was over, what was the final result(s)?

_____

_____

_____

_____

Looking back, could you have done anything differently to glorify God and live consistently according to His character?

_____

_____

_____

_____

As the saying goes, hindsight is always 20-20. But with these lessons in mind, are there any events or situations that are ongoing? What can you do today to be faithful to the revelation of God in your life and ask Him to come and be a part of this trial?

_____

_____

_____

_____

_____

_____

This lesson is a weighty consideration of the sovereignty of God, and how He may at times allow difficulty to come into our lives in order to move us to a closer relationship with Him. The questions asked in this chapter may have caused you to dig deep in your responses. As you think over this chapter and insights you have gained, this point would be a good place to thank God for His sovereign work in your life. Everything God allows is His action to draw you closer to Him. Although it is easy to lose sight of this, God is at work to create a heart like His own out of our own selfish hearts.

Father God,

Thank You for Your love and creative work in my life. Lord, it is so easy to get caught up in my own feelings when life gets difficult, or when I suffer from someone else's unkindness. But God, I see now that You are there in the midst of the trial, drawing me closer to You. Father, thank You for the sunshine and the rain. Thank You for the mountaintop when I feel so close to You, and the valley when it is a struggle to look up. Lord, I know You want me to become more like You. Thank You, and draw me close to Your heart throughout all the events of my life. Amen.

Week Five: Summary

"My son, do not make light of the Lord's discipline, and do not lose heart when he rebukes you, because the Lord disciplines those he loves, and he punishes everyone he accepts as a son." Endure hardship as discipline; God is treating you as sons. For what son is not disciplined by his father? If you are not disciplined (and everyone undergoes discipline), then you are illegitimate children and not true sons. Moreover, we have all had human fathers who disciplined us and we respected them for it. How much more should we submit to the Father of our spirits and live! Our fathers disciplined us for a little while as they thought best; but God disciplines us for our good, that we may share in his holiness.

—Hebrews 12:5b-10

This week's lessons have introduced you to some new ideas about Joseph and the ways in which God worked in his life. What is one new idea that you have learned this week? If there is one thought or idea that God used to grab your attention, write it on the lines below.

_____

_____

_____

_____

_____

_____

_____

_____

_____

_____

Joseph

Joseph in Jail

Hold your peace with me, and let me speak, Then let come on me what may! Why do I take my flesh in my teeth, and put my life in my hands? Though He slay me, yet will I trust Him. Even so, I will defend my own ways before Him. He also shall be my salvation.

—Job 13:13-16a NKJV

Day One: Take a Look at God's Word

From the Broadway stage production of *Joseph and the Amazing Technicolor Dreamcoat* to the flannel-graph images of Sunday school, the story of Joseph has been told, time and again. But as you consider Joseph's life, it is easy to forget the reality of the darkness which he faced. Joseph was a real person, with hopes, thoughts, feelings, and desires, just like yours or mine. He suffered incredible loss when betrayed by his brothers and sold into slavery. For twenty years, Joseph labored in the dark, with no hope that his circumstances would ever change. And then, suddenly, there was a glimmer of light in his dark dungeon cell. God sent dreams to two of Joseph's fellow prisoners and allowed Joseph to understand their meanings.

After fifteen years, this was the first event that tied Joseph's present to his past. The God of his fathers, who had sent Joseph the dreams that had ultimately been responsible for his deportation, was visibly active in Joseph's life again. The baker and the butler were able to find God in the jail cell, because God Himself had placed Joseph there for a greater purpose. Their dreams ignited a hope in Joseph that had all but died.

Genesis 40 is the basis of this story.

Read Genesis 40.

As you read, try to picture the setting from Joseph's perspective, and what he might have learned from his encounter with the king's servants.

Record your thoughts and insights below.

_____

_____

_____

_____

_____

_____

_____

Day Two: The View from the Jail Cell

Morning came early to Joseph's cell. Daylight streamed through the window above his bed, but Joseph had already risen from the stone mattress. After he had spent years in the putrid hole, today was to be different. Today Joseph carried a rekindled hope. He washed his face expectantly in the stone cup that held his day's water ration and shook the dust from his clothes. He then made his rounds up and down the dank prison corridors — his job was to make sure that the inmates were fed and still alive. After his tasks were completed, Joseph checked with the chief jailer and returned to his cell to watch the day's ceremonies through his window. This same routine served as the bookends for Joseph's days. Each morning and evening he was grateful for the hour in which he could be out of his cell, a reprieve from the stone, ten-foot cube within which the entirety of his life existed. But on this day, he returned to his cell filled with expectancy.

The stone window above his bed faced the street level just outside. It was barely large enough for Joseph to get his head into as he stood on his stone bed, but Joseph could view the public market's activities, at least from the perspective of an insect in the dust. This window was the only source of fresh air or light in the dank cell that had been his home for the last four years. Joseph had stood in that very position many times, trying to see past the shuffling feet and animals' hooves. At times he was lost in thought, trying to fend off the crushing fear that he would never again be free. But today things were going to be different.

Thirteen dark years had passed since Joseph's brothers sold him to the Ishmaelite caravan bound for Egypt. His life's path skewed, Joseph became a slave on the auction block in an Egyptian square. He first served in Potiphar's house, and then, because of his godly character and the favor of the Lord, he rose to a position of prominence and responsibility. Then, just as suddenly, he was falsely accused of rape and cast into Pharaoh's prison. But everywhere Joseph went, God was with him, and his integrity was honored and rewarded.

These ordeals had changed him. The painful memories of his youthful arrogance still rang in his ears. The day he stood on the rock and declared his dreams to his brothers haunted him. Had Joseph's own arrogance or God's sovereignty caused his situation? Four years in Pharaoh's prison could have left Joseph hopeless and bitter, but he had remained faithful, and God quietly met him in his faithfulness.

As Joseph stood at the window of his prison cell, he recalled the events that occurred three days prior. Three days ago something familiar had lit the candle of hope in Joseph's heart anew. God's hand appeared again in Joseph's barren existence. He was reminded of his past, yet at the same time the event ignited hope inside his dungeon of despair.

Three days ago Joseph sat with the king's baker and cupbearer as they narrated their troubled dreams. The dreams left the men agitated, but they made perfect sense to Joseph. They reminded Joseph of the dreams of his youth, of his father and his home. The cupbearer recounted to Joseph a vision of three vines that he squeezed into juice and then served to the king. It was clear to Joseph: In three days the cupbearer would be lifted up and redeemed from the prison, and placed back at Pharaoh's side.

This favorable unraveling of his friend's dream gave the baker confidence to share his own dream with Joseph. In it, three baskets of bread perched atop the baker's head were lifted up so high that the birds of the air feasted from them. The baker's countenance brightened as he waited for Joseph's favorable interpretation, but his destiny was not to be pleasant. In three days the baker would also be released from prison, only to be executed. For whatever reason, the whims of the king would not blow favorably toward the baker that day.

As the crowd gathered outside the window, Joseph remembered his last request to the men. "Remember me when these events come to pass," Joseph had pleaded. "This interpretation did not come from me, but from God, who watches over my life. If these events should occur, please remember my name to Pharaoh. Tell him how I have been unjustly held in this prison for years. I only ask to be returned to Pharaoh's service." The baker and the cupbearer both promised to remember. Then they were gone.

Loud shouts of approval brought Joseph's attention back to the courtyard. He couldn't view the stage from his ground-level vantage point, but at the far end of the square Joseph heard Pharaoh's decree releasing the cupbearer and restoring him into service. The crowd applauded the king's mercy. But then the following hush that fell on the crowd was interrupted by the dull thud of the executioner's axe. No one spoke or moved. Minutes later above the hushed crowd, carrion birds circled and squawked over the spectacle. Although Joseph could not see, he knew the dreams he had interpreted just days before had come to pass. Life had come to the cupbearer and death to the baker. In both of these events, Joseph found new hope. He knew that God was still a part of his life. The God he had heard of in stories while sitting on his father's knee, the God of Abraham, the God of Isaac, and the God of his father, Jacob, was still alive! The God who had given him vivid dreams in his youth was still concerned about his life. Joseph believed that the next day would be his last day in the dark prison cell. *Surely the cupbearer will remember my name. When the excitement of this day has come and gone, and the cupbearer is returned to service, he will remember me — how I interpreted his dream with the hand of God — and I will be released.*

That night Joseph slept little on his stone mattress. He tossed and turned, discovering again how many vermin crawled in and out of his cell in the dark. The rancid smells attracted them to this foul place. Joseph looked up to heaven and prayed, *Thank You, God, for releasing me from this place. Thank You for hearing my cry after these many long years. Thank You that tomorrow will be the day I return to freedom. Perhaps I will even be able to leave this country soon and return to my father's house.*

Joseph arose early the next morning. During his rounds, he checked on the prisoners. The shackled were still shackled...the unbound were still in their cells. He delivered their rations of bread and water. On the lower level Joseph discovered two more lifeless bodies. These cells were dark, without windows like the one Joseph enjoyed. Only shadows cast from the eerie torch light filtered into the rooms, so Joseph couldn't see the corpses, but the pungent odor told him that life had left these poor men many hours earlier. He summoned the guard and notified the burial detail. As Joseph returned to his cell, he told the chief jailer that there were two more rooms available — not that the availability of accommodations mattered as to how many people were thrown into this rancid hole in the ground, but Joseph still remembered the beatings he received when he hadn't kept the jailer informed.

Joseph returned to his room and waited for the cupbearer's return. Once again he shook out his clothes. He was certain that at any moment, the wooden door at the end of the hall would creak open, and his name would be called. How Joseph longed for just a pitcher of water to wash the dust from his face. How could he go to Pharaoh soaked in the prison smells? Lunchtime came, and evening slowly fell. Joseph patiently watched the shadow from his window creep across the floor, and then up the wall until it faded to nothingness. No messenger came that day. The next morning, and the next, and the next all came and left Joseph with no callers.

Weeks crawled past, and finally Joseph arose to his knees in the early morning shadows. He was ready to explode with broken desires. *Father God, why have You forsaken me? Have I been unfaithful to You? All I want is to return to my father's house. Please, God, help the cupbearer remember my name today!* Joseph collapsed into a broken heap, weeping on the floor. He lay there, groaning like a dying animal until he barely had strength to breathe. Visions of his father, his mother, stepmothers, and brothers flooded his mind. He no longer held bitterness toward his brothers. He only wanted to return home, to be released and find peace in his father's tents. *Father God, I don't understand why all this has happened to me. I am a stranger in a strange land. My only comfort is Your presence...and the memory of my father...in this foul place. God of Abraham, Isaac, and my father, Jacob, hear my cry, and release me today.*

While God had orchestrated these events, the final brush strokes that would complete the portrait of God's character had not yet been painted on Joseph's canvas. God was not ready, and no one knocked on Joseph's door that day. The concrete heavens remained silent.

From our elevated perspective safe on the tower of time, we know that Joseph's cries were eventually answered. God sent the Pharaoh a disturbing dream, and while searching for interpreters, the cupbearer remembered a man named Joseph in the dungeons. Not knowing if Joseph was even still alive, he spoke to the king, and Joseph was released — not to return to his father's house, but to ascend to a position of leadership and authority in the Egyptian kingdom. God had personally begun to fulfill the vision He had given Joseph two decades earlier.

Have you ever cried out for an answer from God, only to feel the heavens return a silent stare? You know that God is there. He has answered your prayers before. You have friends who have received miracles, but for some reason on that day you have nothing but memories. When God embraces you with the silence of the desert trial, His purpose is to replace your own stubbornness with His character. God must prepare our hearts before He can reveal Himself in a deeper way and complete His plan in our lives.

Psalm 71:18-22 (KJV) says this:

> Now also when I am old and greyheaded, O God, forsake me not; until I have shewed thy strength unto this generation, and thy power to every one that is to come. Thy righteousness also, O God, is very high, who hast done great things: O God, who is like unto thee! Thou, which hast shewed me great and sore troubles, shalt quicken me again, and shalt bring me up again from the depths of the earth. Thou shalt increase my greatness, and comfort me on every side. I will also praise thee with the psaltery, even thy truth, O my God: unto thee will I sing with the harp, O thou Holy One of Israel.

God's purpose in every event in your life is to prepare you to be a vessel through which He can reveal His glory to the world. The next principle in this process is as follows:

Principle Six: God will often use the desert of quiet faithful service, or the prison of injustice, to permanently transform our self-confidence into Christ-confidence. It is only when control is out of our own hands and we are thrust blindly into God's arms that He is free to teach us that He can be completely relied upon.

How have you seen principle six demonstrated in your own life?

_____

_____

_____

_____

_____

Day Three: God's Sovereignty and Your Suffering

The revelation of God's faithfulness that transforms your character cannot happen without your willing cooperation. Day by day, you make decisions to obey God and follow His principles. At other times, this process begins in spite of our unwillingness, but until you surrender to God's quiet purposes, life remains unchanged. Like Joseph, when control is taken from your hands, God is at work teaching you that you can trust in Him. In the midst of the joy, laughter, pain or difficulty that frame the different seasons of your life, the heavens may seem to be silent when you need most to hear His reassuring voice. You may not understand. Doubts may haunt your soul. Why, at a time when you desperately need Him, has He apparently abandoned you? When the silence of heaven becomes deafening, God is still at work filling your heart with more of Himself. God is building His character in you through the difficulty, rather than by rescuing you from it.

This process is not limited to Joseph's life in the Old Testament. The writer of Hebrews tells us that even Jesus — God's own Son — was put through the process of difficulty and trials in order to learn from His Father's hands. Hebrews 5:8-9 says this:

> *Although he was a son, he learned obedience from what he suffered and, once made perfect, he became the source of eternal salvation for all who obey him.*

Paul writes in 2 Corinthians 1:3-5:

> *Praise be to the God and Father of our Lord Jesus Christ, the Father of compassion and the God of all comfort, who comforts us in all our troubles, so that we can comfort those in any trouble with the comfort we ourselves have received from God.*

The gift of tribulation can be God's blessing. God's purpose is that you will become more like Him and learn to draw from the resources which obedience makes available. There are no biblical promises that guarantee a peaceful, pain-free life. But throughout Scripture, God promises to be with you in every difficulty. As you read through the following verses, ask yourself how these scriptures could apply to your life — in the situations that you are facing today.

Throughout Scripture, God promises that He will:

Rescue those who call on Him.

Psalm 145:18-19

2 Samuel 22:4-7, 20

How could this apply to your own life?

_____

_____

Protect those who come to Him.

Psalm 18:1-6

How could this apply to your own life?

_____

_____

Pursue those who run from Him.

Psalm 139

How could this apply to your own life?

_____

_____

Strengthen those who are weak.

Psalm 73:24-26

Isaiah 40:29-31

How could this apply to your own life?

_____

_____

Be a Provider in times of need.

Habakkuk 3:17-19

How could this apply to your own life?

_____

_____

Be a Friend to the friendless.

Psalm 25:16-22

Psalm 34:22

How could this apply to your own life?

_____

_____

Be a Help to the helpless.

Psalm 10:14

Psalm 54:4

How could this apply to your own life?

_____

_____

Be a Deliverer in times of trouble.

Genesis 14:20

Psalm 18:1-3

How could this apply to your own life?

_____

_____

Give new life to those who call on Him with a pure heart.

Psalm 24:3-5

Jeremiah 24:7

How could this apply to your own life?

_____

_____

The unspoken assumption in these promises is that you are likely to experience weakness, friendlessness, helplessness, trouble, and despair. There will be times in your life when you need to be protected, to be rescued, or to find a friend. But God's promises are sure: He will meet your needs.

As you finish your Bible study time today, take a moment and ask yourself this question: What do you expect from God in your life? What provisions do you expect from Him?

There are times when your own unmet expectations can be the source of the greatest disruptions in your spiritual walk. If you expect your ship to be guided away from troubled water, but you still sail into storm after storm, it can become distressing! If you expect constant times of peace but instead experience turbulent times, you may begin to assume that God is either on a coffee break, that He doesn't care about you, or that maybe you did something to deserve the trouble.

In your own walk with God, what are your expectations?

_____

_____

_____

How are they currently being met?

_____

_____

_____

Measure these expectations against God's Word, and against what you have learned so far from the lives of David and Joseph.

How are your expectations in alignment or disagreement with God's Word? Refer to today's verses or examples from Scripture to back up your answer.

_____

_____

_____

_____

_____

_____

Day Four: The Quietness of the Desert Night

Does the Bible make promises that your ship will always stay in the warm, crystal-blue waters of a glassy summer sea? God does not promise continual peace in outward circumstances, but He does promise to give us the "peace that passes all human understanding" — in the midst of every situation He allows into our lives. The difficult situations often come from His hands in order to crack open our selfish hearts to His redeeming grace. God will do whatever He deems necessary to prepare you for a life that can glorify Him. And a life that glorifies Him will spring from a heart that has learned to trust Him at all times.

This period we have investigated in Joseph's life lasted over two decades. He moved from the favorite son in his father's household, to one of many held captive in a slave caravan, to a servant in Potiphar's household. But because of his faithfulness, God responded by giving him responsibility and recognition. Then injustice again leapt from the shadows, and Joseph was thrown into the Egyptian prison. After God rekindled the flame of hope in Joseph's life through the butler and baker's dreams, the heavens seemed to remain cruelly silent yet again. Joseph's answer was delayed for two more years. During this entire time, God was at work, and when Joseph was ready on the inside — in his heart — then God was ready to act on the outside — in his circumstances.

"God Must Want Me To..."

What about difficulties in your own life? Periods of desert trial and heavenly silence come into every growing Christian's life. How you respond determines when and how God will release the answers to your prayers. Sometimes when the heavens are silent, the natural response is to fabricate your own solution. Your prayers haven't been answered, so you manufacture your own. "It must be God wants me to do this" is a refrain that echoes across the pages of Scripture.

Aaron rationalized the smelting of a golden calf because Moses had been on the mountain longer than he liked, and his presumption led the nation of Israel into idolatry. During the era of the judges, the nation of Israel was described this way: *Everyone did what was right in his own eyes* (Judges 21:25 NKJV). The results are always disastrous when you take God's will into your own hands. We will look at two such examples of "entrepreneurial praying" in upcoming weeks' studies.

The lesson behind these events is that when you take God's work into your own hands, you will likely create a mess! When God is silent to your cries for His assistance, He is not testing your resourcefulness. He is waiting for you to surrender.

Are there events in your life that fit this model? You have prayed and prayed. And in the absence of an answer, you set out on your own journey. "God must want me to…" you say. These are decisions that mold your heart, to either make you more amenable to the Spirit's leading, or more self-willed, opposed to God's ultimate desires in your life.

Are there events in your life that follow the pattern of the phrase, "God must want me to…"? Write your thoughts below.

_____

_____

_____

_____

_____

In the New Testament, God displays the same apparent lack of concern for devoted Christians' prayers — but He is teaching His people the lesson of utter reliance on Him. John 11:1-45 tells the story of Lazarus' death and resurrection. Jesus was notified that His friend Lazarus was sick, and with the reputation Jesus had for healing, his sisters thought Jesus would come to Lazarus' aid immediately. But God had a different agenda than the healing of just one man. God's agenda was to glorify Himself and to draw many others into the revelation of His love.

According to Jesus' words in John 11:14-15, what were His thoughts and feelings about His friend's death?

_____

_____

_____

_____

When Martha challenged Jesus on His delay, how did Jesus reply? (verses 21-27)

_____

_____

What was the focus of Jesus' prayer just before He called Lazarus out of the tomb?

_____

_____

Jesus was moved by his friends' grief, and He cried with them in sorrow over His friend's death. But Jesus' purpose was directed not at relieving their immediate feelings of loss. Instead Jesus focused on giving His friends a revelation of Himself and the Father's love that they would never forget.

Lazarus had been dead for three days. The family had undoubtedly prepared Lazarus' body for a traditional burial, which meant a homeopathic embalming. A dead body would be wrapped in layers of linens and spices that had been mixed into a self-hardening paste. Not only had Lazarus been dead for three days, but it would have been physically impossible for him to get up and walk across his tomb to the door even if he were alive. So when Lazarus came out of the tomb wrapped head to toe in over seventy-five pounds of spices and linens, the people gathered there knew beyond a shadow of a doubt that Jesus was Lord of the living and the dead. His power extended beyond healing diseases; all of life was subject to His word.

Look at the event(s) you described in the lines above regarding "filling in the blanks" of God's will ("God must want me to..."). What was the result of your spiritual entrepreneurialism?

_____

_____

_____

_____

What did you hope that God would do?

_____

_____

_____

Are there steps you can take right now to put these circumstances back into God's hands and allow Him to fulfill His own redemptive purposes in your life?

_____

_____

_____

If there is a situation brewing in your life, or the life of your friends that you can commit to the Lord, write your prayer of consecration and surrender in the lines below before moving onto the second half of today's lesson.

_____

_____

_____

_____

"God, How Can You...?"

When night falls over the open seas, sailors look to the heavens and guide their course by the stars. But when the silence of heaven descends on your journey, even the stars can become obscured. Without a tangible sense of God's constant presence, the disconcerting feeling that God has abandoned you can arise, and like waves on the open sea, these feelings may seek to capsize your boat. Even when God seems far away, He has promised that He will never leave or forsake you. Even in the deepest darkness, the same God who watched over Joseph is watching over you. He is never absent, and God is seldom inactive. During the time when Joseph felt he was languishing in jail, God was preparing Joseph for His purposes.

You can respond to God's silence by becoming angry, sullen, bitter or even depressed. You may want to give up while God waits for you to surrender. But the pathway out of a desert is to surrender to His will, to surrender to the circumstances, to say, _Yes, God, I will serve You here, regardless of any change that I see._

When your heart can finally let go of demanding your own solutions, then God will bring the results that you have longed for and His answers to your prayers. By the time you surrender, God has changed your heart, melted your proud attitude, and tempered your self-will so that you are ready to joyfully say, _Father, Your will be done._

God's plan is all about redemption. Even if you take yourself out of His perfect plan for your life, He will bring the opportunity back to you to follow His will. The Israelites were ready to leave Egypt when Moses led them out of their slavery. Four hundred years of slavery in a foreign land had certainly created the will to leave. But the first time they stood on the banks of the Jordan River just a few weeks later, they did not have the will to go forward into what God had called them to. For the next forty years the Israelites wandered in the desert until the doubters died, and the entire nation was ready to follow God's plan in faith. Forty years later, the same nation stood in the same place, and God asked them to make the same decision.

In the New Testament, we would not have the gospel of Mark had it not been for God's redemptive love. Mark was traveling with Paul and Barnabas on their first missionary journey. According to Acts 13:13, the missionary life proved to be too difficult for the young man, and he deserted them on the first return ship to Jerusalem. According to Acts 15:38, Paul held on to his disappointment regarding Mark, and did not want him to join the group for their second journey. The division was so severe that Paul and Barnabas went separate directions. It was not until the end of Paul's third missionary journey that he wrote to the Colossian church and to Timothy that Mark had rejoined the group, and that he was "profitable for the ministry" (see Colossians 4:10 and 2 Timothy 4:11).

For a time, Mark took himself out of the game. His attitude prevented him from contributing to the work of spreading the gospel. We are not told whether it was fear of rejection, fear of failure, a disagreement with Paul or some other reason behind Mark's departure. But the story does show us that God is a redeemer. On the cross He saved us from sin. In our final moments He will save us from eternal death. During our lives, He saves us from ourselves.

Can you relate to the Israelites or to Mark's negative attitudes? If so, in what way? In what ways has God given you a second chance?

_____

_____

_____

_____

_____

_____

Day Five: Finding God's Purpose in the Wilderness

Joseph was a type of Christ. He was a foreshadowing of the Savior who would rise up to redeem God's people. Just as Joseph went into the dungeon to arise to rule, so Jesus went to the cross, and the grave, only to arise to rule and lead His people to an eternal salvation. Joseph was a type of Christ, and God took the time to form his character and heart before he was released into his ministry. You and I are called to imitate Christ and to minister to the world around us. Therefore, we can expect that God will work in our lives to create tender hearts and godly character through which He can work *before* we will have an expanded influence in the lives of others.

Joseph was not completely aware of God's plan during the time he was being prepared for the throne. Joseph didn't receive the confirmation of his dreams until his brothers came looking for food a decade later. But as Christians today, we *can* know what direction Jesus is leading us.

The Beatitudes listed in Matthew 5 are some of the character traits that God wants to see cultivated in your life and mine. These qualities may seem elusive to us, but they describe the kind of life that Jesus lived. When life deals us an unjust hand, the mirage of godly character often vanishes on the horizon. These ten verses outline the very character traits God is seeking to sculpt out of our selfishness.

Blessed are the poor in spirit, for theirs is the kingdom of heaven.

Blessed are those who mourn, for they will be comforted.

Blessed are the meek, for they will inherit the earth.

Blessed are those who hunger and thirst for righteousness, for they will be filled.

Blessed are the merciful, for they will be shown mercy.

Blessed are the pure in heart, for they will see God.

Blessed are the peacemakers, for they will be called sons of God.

Blessed are those who are persecuted because of righteousness, for theirs is the kingdom of heaven.

Blessed are you when people insult you, persecute you and falsely say all kinds of evil against you because of me. Rejoice and be glad, because great is your reward in heaven, for in the same way they persecuted the prophets who were before you.

—Verses 3-12

In this passage, Jesus lists eight specific traits that will bring blessing into your life. So many times when we hear sermons about "bringing blessing into our lives," the subjects revolve around giving to the church, praying extensive prayers, or standing on the promises of God. How many sermons do you hear about asking God to bring you into mourning, so that you can experience His comfort? Do you hear sermons about desperately hungering and thirsting for righteousness, so that you can experience God as He fills those desires? No, our prayers often ascend from a selfish heart, one that prays in order to receive a blessing.

These verses outline a life of one who prays in order to bless God and be a conduit of His influence in the world. The blessing that comes in such a person's life is a more complete manifestation of God's character.

Take a few minutes and meditate on Matthew 5:3-12. Which of these qualities can you select and specifically apply to your life and actions right now? When you do so, you are taking steps that are pleasing to God and will further His plan in your life.

Listed below are the eight characteristics from the Beatitudes. On the lines provided, describe in detail how you could bring these elements into your life. Many of these characteristics will only become a part of your life as you identify yourself more completely with the cause of Christ and become an agent of change for Him in the culture around you. For example, you will never be persecuted for righteousness' sake if you do not choose to live an outwardly counter-cultural Christian life.

On these lines, describe how you can participate with God in fostering each character trait in your life.

Poor in spirit

_____

_____

_____

Mournful

_____

_____

_____

Meek

_____

_____

_____

Hungering for righteousness

_____

_____

_____

Merciful

_____

_____

_____

Pure in heart

_____

_____

_____

Being a peacemaker

_____

_____

_____

Persecuted for the sake of righteousness

_____

_____

_____

It's likely that as you look back at the events you described in this chapter, you can see a pattern beginning to emerge. Our God is a God of order, and if there are one or two specific traits He is trying to build into your life, His work will point to a common theme. It may be that everywhere you turn, you are being confronted with opportunities to talk about Christ. It may be that everything in your life seems to be falling apart, and you just want to see God's presence in the midst of it all. It may be that you have been faithful in your decisions, and the joy you feel is the fruit of becoming pure in heart. If there are one or two of these characteristics which you most want to see in your life, or already see most active in your life, what would they be?

On the lines below, specifically describe how these eight characteristics are, or can be, at work to change your life.

_____

_____

_____

_____

_____

In Joseph's life, God pursued the formation of these characteristics through difficulties and trials. What about you? Can you remember a time when the heavens were silent in your life, and the circumstances moved you to plead for a sign from above? Note some of the details of that experience below.

_____

_____

_____

_____

_____

What were your attitudes or actions? What were your feelings as you lived through these times? How did you respond to the unexpected change in your life's course?

_____

_____

_____

_____

Maybe you're still in the middle of a desert of quiet preparation in your life. Have your decisions distanced you from God's purposes? The issue is not fairness, or justice, or even who is right or wrong. Because God's purpose is to create His heart within you, the issue is how you are responding to the situations God is allowing. Maybe you haven't been able to let go of a sour attitude, brought on because God didn't respond in the way that you wanted.

What are some of your thoughts and feelings revolving around these events in your life?

_____

_____

_____

> *A man's pride shall bring him low: but honour shall uphold the humble in spirit.*
> —Proverbs 29:23 KJV

> *God opposes the proud but gives grace to the humble.*
> —James 4:6

Taking God's character into your heart is not a complicated intellectual process. It doesn't become a part of your life because you follow religious rituals or participate in your church's sacraments. The rituals and sacraments we enjoy in our church life are an important part of our Christian heritage and traditions. But allowing God to change your heart comes down to one simple decision: When your desires are pulling at you to respond in self-interest and put yourself ahead of God or others, will you resist or give in? When Jesus said that we must take up our cross and follow Him, He wasn't referring to outward religious formalities, going without specific foods, or dressing in approved clothing. He wants to know if you will deny what you want, and choose instead to pursue what He wants for you. He put no qualifiers on this request, such as:

• If it's not too much trouble…

• As long as you don't get embarrassed…

• If it doesn't interfere with your career…

• As long as your family understands…

Jesus only asks that you obey Him. At times, we have the choice. At other times, God engineers the circumstances in such a way that our choices are limited. But always God moves to teach us more of His grace, mercy, and love.

When you don't respond to God's invitation to become more like Him, the culprit blocking your path is likely pride. Even when circumstances are beyond your control, pride can unwillingly block the path toward becoming more Christ-like. Like a tap-rooted dandelion that refuses to give up its hold on the earth, pride is a final anchor to self-will. (And like the unfriendly weed, it has ways of coming back.) When you hold on to your pride, your "right" to a better situation, unforgiveness is a likely byproduct. A bitter attitude is only pride wrapped up in a self-righteous covering.

You may be hurt over something that "should have" gone your way. You may be indignant because of the way someone treated you. Doesn't this attitude really say, *I should have had it my way. Now I'm upset that I didn't get it my way, and I have a right to be upset!* God opposes this attitude, and you place yourself in opposition to Him when you hold on to these corrupting emotions. Is that really how you want to live? Consider the events you have described in the previous pages, and fill in your thoughts on the following lines.

How are you responding to difficult or unjust circumstances?

_____

_____

_____

From whom are you seeking attention with your efforts?

_____

_____

What is really important in this situation?

_____

_____

_____

The greater question is, what is God asking from you? This is a much different question than, "What can I give God?" or "What can I do for God at this point in time?" What is *the Lord* asking from you? Is it just to sit in quiet praise and accept His hand? Is it to rejoice in the tribulation in which you're immersed? Your circumstances may be something over which you have absolutely no control. Just as Joseph shuffled behind the Ishmaelites' caravan through the sand and prayed on the dungeon's dirt floor, you too can experience the power of God in the midst of the situation.

What is God asking of you in the situation you have described?

_____

_____

_____

Which beatitude applies to this situation? Which characteristic of a godly heart will you apply to your situation, beginning today? Your answer here may not be the one that will bring an immediate solution. But your answer can begin a course of action that will release God to work in your circumstances.

_____

_____

_____

_____

This simple decision may seem like a small thing. But when you change an attitude that you have been holding on to, you will likely change an associated action. And when you change an action, you begin to build new habits that will change your character. When you voluntarily bring your life into harmony with God's character and purposes for your life, you release God to work in the midst of your circumstances.

Through this process, you become what Jesus called you to be in the verses just following the Beatitudes in His Sermon on the Mount:

> *"You are the salt of the earth. But if the salt loses its saltiness, how can it be made salty again? It is no longer good for anything, except to be thrown out and trampled by men. You are the light of the world. A city on a hill cannot be hidden. Neither do people light a lamp and put it under a bowl. Instead they put it on its stand, and it gives light to everyone in the house. In the same way, let your light shine before men, that they may see your good deeds and praise your Father in heaven.*
> —Matthew 5:13-16

If the event on which you have been reflecting is a situation that happened in the past, on the lines below, recall and give praise to God for what He did when you surrendered it and released Him to work in your life. If this is a circumstance in which you are still immersed, and you don't see any answers, take a minute and write a prayer in the lines below. Ask God to bring about the changes in your heart that He desires to bring. Then ask Him to bring His results and glorify Himself through your life in this difficult situation.

_____

_____

_____

_____

_____

_____

_____

_____

_____

_____

Father God,

Life can be so unfair at times. And when it is, I want to respond back in the same way. "An eye for an eye, and a tooth for a tooth," isn't that what You said? Yes, revenge is one way of responding to my own broken emotions, but Lord, You call me to respond differently. You call me to find peace in Your hands even if the world is assaulting my peace. You call me to be someone who loves at all times, even when the world is filled with hate. And by allowing You to flow through my life in this way, Lord, I will look for You to change my world and work through me to bring others to You. Jesus, help me in my weakness. Help me find the courage to be merciful, to long for righteousness, and to be a peacemaker, a representative of Your kingdom to my family, to my friends, and to the world. Thank You. In Jesus' name. Amen.

Week Six: Summary

For the grace of God that bringeth salvation hath appeared to all men, Teaching us that, denying ungodliness and worldly lusts, we should live soberly, righteously, and godly, in this present world; Looking for that blessed hope, and the glorious appearing of the great God and our Saviour Jesus Christ; Who gave himself for us, that he might redeem us from all iniquity, and purify unto himself a peculiar people, zealous of good works.

—Titus 2:11-14 KJV

This week's lessons have introduced you to some new ideas about Joseph and the ways in which God worked in his life. What is one new idea that you have learned this week? If there is one thought or idea that God used to grab your attention, write it on the lines below.

_____

_____

_____

_____

_____

Joseph

WEEK SEVEN

In the Halls of Justice

Mercy and truth preserve the king: and his throne is upholden by mercy.

—Proverbs 20:28 KJV

Day One: Take a Look at God's Word

Joseph disappeared from his family as a teen, and emerged as a ruler in the most powerful kingdom in the world at that time, second in power only to Pharaoh himself. Throughout this time, God never deserted him, nor did Joseph's faithfulness to his father's God wane. What changed inside of Joseph's heart to prepare him for this day? God prepared him for a position that would alter history by personally molding his character through suffering and trials.

This week we move to the climax of Joseph's life. His brothers are unaware as they entered the great hall that they would soon be bowing before their lost brother. And Joseph had all but given up on his dreams. God chose these circumstances in Joseph's life through which He would reveal Himself, and God often chooses to intersect your life through circumstances equally as bleak.

Read Genesis 41:33 through Genesis 42:38. Reflect on how God demonstrated His faithfulness throughout the span of Joseph's life. Record your thoughts below.

_____

_____

_____

_____

_____

_____

_____

_____

When your ability to fulfill God's will in your life is gone, God is free to work. When you know that you cannot take credit for His doings, God is free to bless you and knows that His blessings will flow through you to others. When God promised the Israelites a homeland, it was a land overflowing with milk and honey. When He supplied manna and quail in the desert, there was plenty for everyone. When Jesus blessed a few fish and loaves of bread and then broke them to feed the crowds, His followers picked up bushels of supplies even after everyone had eaten their fill. The issue is never the ability of God to supply your needs. The issue is the condition of our hearts, whether we will allow God to be glorified in our lives or keep God's blessings for ourselves. Are we faithful or foolish? Merciful or unforgiving? Do we glorify ourselves with God's gifts or glorify God?

Write your thoughts about Joseph's life and your attitudes in your own prayers below.

_____

_____

_____

_____

_____

_____

_____

_____

_____

Day Two: Walking in Joseph's Footsteps

Joseph met the desert dawn as he strolled through the pristine palace corridors. As the new ruler over Egypt's expanding grain reserves and merchants, he checked the gates and admitted the small horde of gaggling merchants. Each morning, Joseph opened the gates to these spirited Bedouin hagglers. They filled the courtyard outside of Pharaoh's palace with carts of lush fruits and other colorful foods from their own towns. The commotion rose with the dust, and before the sun popped over the palace walls, an empty courtyard had been transformed into one of the richest bazaars in all of Egypt. The shouts from men selling melons, rugs, and exotic spices filled the courtyard, echoing off the stone walls.

By the time the sun illuminated the walls of the market, the square was bursting with citizenry, tradesmen, and vendors, all showcasing delicacies from their homelands. Three of the seven years of famine that Joseph predicted had come and gone. But because of God's wisdom operating in Joseph's life, Egypt had not only conserved food for itself, but they had surplus to sell to natives of the Nile and beyond.

God's provision is always more than enough, Joseph thought. He recalled twenty-three years of God's provision through dungeons, as a servant and a jailer. Still, God's mercy had not changed. Because God had chosen to bless Joseph and bring him into a place of authority, God also had chosen to bless Egypt. Each month it seemed that more and more vendors brought their caravans in from the east and the south. They set up their tents, carts, and tables in the courtyard. A few months ago, Joseph had bought fine purple linen for his wife and jewels for Pharaoh's jubilee. He loved the unique treasures and hid them in the folds of his robes as a surprise for his children.

As Joseph meandered through the market square, he was stopped by two old women. The clothes were worn but skillfully mended. They had ventured in from a region south of Goshen, and they bowed low before the magistrate. Thanking him for the food they bartered, one said, "Our village had no food, and most of the bark had been stripped from the trees for soup. Even the water was beginning to dry in the river beds." In the palace market they found everything for which they had prayed. They thanked Joseph, and they thanked their gods for Joseph's foresight and preparation. Joseph watched them shuffle away, weaving between the carts and wares. *God of my father, Jacob, and of his fathers, Isaac and Abraham, You are always faithful,* Joseph prayed quietly as he stood under the hot desert sky.

As he paused to wipe the moisture from his eyes, Joseph realized that he stood in front of a small, half-moon-shaped window that was hewn through the wall just above the dusty market streets. This was the dungeon window through which he had peered for so many sleepless nights. He had watched as the butler was reinstated to the king's service, and as the baker met his own fate. Joseph paused to consider the events of the past twenty-three years. He still desired to see his family, but now he had a family of his own. He still yearned for closure, if there were such a thing, with the hostile brothers who had sold him into slavery. More than anything, he dreamed to see his father, Jacob. *Is he still alive, or has the desert taken its toll on my father's life?*

Joseph remembered the nights he pushed his head through the half-moon stone portal just to glimpse the stars. How he had prayed for God to let him go home. The heavens didn't answer, at least, not in the way he had expected. So much had transpired since that day…. He still yearned for his family, but no longer was consumed by the unfulfilled quest. God had blessed him. God had given him purpose and a vision for the success of Egypt. Because Joseph was faithful to that vision, God had blessed him, and all of Egypt as well.

The wealth and commerce generated by the vendors did not escape the pharaoh's eye. As the market became a viable enterprise, Pharaoh had enacted a small tax. "Why should my kingdom go unrewarded for providing these hagglers a place for their wares?" Pharaoh had commented to Joseph one day as they enjoyed the sunrise together. So a small percentage each day was exacted from vendors as they closed their carts, and Pharaoh gave half of this levy to Joseph. Nonetheless, Joseph checked the tax collectors regularly. No one was to exact more than was required. The marketers respected the leader of Egypt for his fairness. This was not the kindness they had been shown in other marketplaces.

As Joseph pondered his life, the sounds and dust of the market drifted away. He could see his father's tent and his mother cooking meals. Only the oppressive heat of the desert sun, which had climbed high overhead, slowly pulled him back to the present day. It was time to close the tables and carts until the afternoon sun danced through its apex. He turned for home with the trinkets and figs in his robe pockets and looked forward to a quiet lunch with his family in the great hall of the palace.

As Joseph and his family reclined in the cool shade of the palace hall, he felt greatly blessed by his wife and children. He had named his firstborn Manasseh, because, as he said, "God has made me to forget my troubles and the troubles of my father's house." Joseph named his second son Ephraim for, he said, "God has made me fruitful in this land of my affliction." Yes, Joseph had a purpose. He had a new vision. The dreams of his youth had not been forgotten, but Joseph had put them to the back of his mind, passing them off as the arrogant desires of a youth in a difficult situation.

After the figs were gone and the table cleared, Joseph played hide-and-seek with Manasseh and Ephraim among the towering columns in the great hall. He knew the gates outside were closing, so he didn't expect any visitors until after the heat had passed. But just as they were ready to start another game, the court crier announced that Joseph had one last group of visitors, a group of shepherds…ten men from the East. They had come looking for food. Joseph was surprised that a group of herdsmen would venture out in such heat. Surely they knew better than to travel under the unyielding midday sun.

As he summoned for them, Joseph ascended the golden throne at the far end of the long marble hall. The hall's limestone floor had consumed a decade of artisan's labor during its construction. The walls in the great hall were carved of gopher wood and cedar, and sandalwood incense floated among its columns. The desert sun beat so intensely that day that it too had crept into the cool of the great hall. But as Joseph's visitors, the ten men from the East, entered through the great arched doorway, the sights and sounds which were his familiar home fled in disbelief.

The oldest of the men looked exactly like his brother Reuben. *Ten herdsmen from the East. Could this be?* Joseph wondered. He quickly roped and tied his emotions. Even if these were the brothers he had longed to see, he would not bless arrogant and vengeful men. As Joseph choked on words he had longed to speak for years, he called out for his interpreter to speak to the men. He asked them where they were from and what their needs were.

Judah stepped forward. "My lord," he said, bowing low, "we are your servants, the son of one man. We come from the East, from the land of Canaan, east of the Great Sea. The famine has reached our land. We have come to buy food to return to our family so that we don't starve."

Of all the days Joseph had suffered, this moment was the most formidable of his life. All of his doubts about his childhood visions vanished as he remembered the dreams of his brothers' sheaves of grain bowing down before his own. God had been faithful to Joseph through injustice, through the scourge of bitter, thankless service, and through years of slavery. Falsely accused, Joseph futilely attempted to forget the years he spent in Pharaoh's putrid prison. Now...here under the desert sun...twenty-three years later, Joseph's brothers didn't recognize him as they bowed low asking the lord of this nation for food. Even though Joseph had given up on his dreams, God had not.

Joseph coated his demeanor with a hardened shell to hide the seething turmoil in his heart. Through his interpreter he accused the men of being spies. He declared that there would be no food that day. They were to leave his land at once and never return again — unless they brought their youngest brother with them. His interpreter conducted them out of the hall and into the courtyard, and then closed and sealed the doors behind them. Joseph could contain himself no longer. He signaled for his butler and even his children to leave. As the door closed at the other end of the great hall, the only sounds that could be heard were Joseph's uncontrolled sobs as he wept again at the faithfulness of his God.

The years he had spent longing for his family had replaced the anger in his heart with love. These feelings, and a flood of thoughts cascaded into his mind. *Have I truly forgiven my brothers? Have they forgiven me? There were only ten. Where is Benjamin? Is he still alive? My father, how is he? And the rest of their children? Surely they have grown into their own clans by this time.*

Joseph longed to see them all, yet his years of suffering had taught him many lessons about the responsibilities of leading. He had seen leaders rise, only to cruelly squash those whom they led as they themselves prospered. He had seen unfaithful servants go unpunished for years, and faithful slaves brutally castigated at the whims of their masters. He had seen men of weak character crumble under their assigned responsibilities, falling under the debilitating weight of their own pride. Joseph understood these things from the suffering that had come into his own life. There was no consistent pattern among men and their fickle desires. The only true thread that ran throughout the events of his life was God's faithfulness. The question Joseph wanted to answer was whether his brothers had learned to bow to God, to allow Him to influence their decisions and shape their character.

So today, in Joseph's court, whether or not a man filled his stomach was not nearly as important as the kind of life he lived. Joseph considered his brothers' request under the uncompromising light of twenty-three years of God's promises. He knew that whether a man sleeps on a soft feather mattress or on a rock slab among the jailhouse rats, the true difference between them lay in how a man treated his neighbor, and what filled his heart.

Joseph drifted for hours, awash on a sea of emotions. The rudder was loose, and the ropes that tied the sails snapped wildly in the wind. He desperately wanted to bless his brothers and see his family again. Yet he had been born to serve faithfully, regardless of his own desires. And that leads us to the next principle:

Principle Seven: Only after we pass tests in the pit of pride, the plateaus of faithful service, and the prison of injustice, and we demonstrate proof of our character through our decisions, are we ready to receive God's promises. If we stray from this character-smelting process, it is possible to delay or completely abort the great revelations of God's character and faithfulness that He has planned to reveal through us.

What is your initial response to this event in Joseph's life? Record your thoughts and feelings below.

_____

_____

_____

_____

_____

Do you agree or disagree with Joseph's actions? Why or why not?

_____

_____

_____

_____

What events in your own life come to mind as you reflect on Joseph's reaction to seeing his brothers?

_____

_____

_____

_____

_____

_____

_____

_____

_____

Day Three: Watching God At Work

God is always at work. In Joseph's life and yours, God was, and still is, perpetually at work. However, your own attitudes and character can keep you from being a part of what God is doing. Joseph was given a specific promise when he was a young teenage boy. God then spent more than twenty years preparing his heart, character, and abilities to be able to fully receive the answer to that promise. Only when he was ready, and when God's timing was perfect, did his brothers walk through the door of Pharaoh's great hall and bow before him. And at that time, Joseph received everything that he had been promised by God. Ultimately, Joseph realized that the purpose of this fulfilled promise was not to glorify himself, but so that he could glorify God. The same truth governs God's purposes in your life today.

God is at work. He is at work in your life and in your church. If you are a part of that effort, then you can understand the incredible revelation of God's love that met Joseph when his brothers walked into the great hall that hot afternoon. If you have not come to that place yet, this lesson can move you toward a deeper understanding of God's faithfulness.

Reflect on the events in Joseph's life in light of your own life's path. What are the lessons you have learned so far this week? Record your thoughts below.

_____

_____

_____

_____

A close friend of mine told me of a struggle that recently developed in his church, and it illustrates this principle in a more contemporary setting. Max's church had flourished under the leadership of one dynamic pastor for more than fifteen years. The church was full every Sunday morning, and nearly full on Sunday and Wednesday nights. After a decade of success, a committee was formed to investigate the option of relocating. Much of their growth had come from the suburbs, and the church's existing facilities were landlocked in their urban neighborhood. After much prayer, committee meetings, and considerable hoopla, the congregation decided to pioneer a daughter church rather than build a new facility.

A portion of the congregation was disappointed by the decision and decided to switch to suburban churches closer to their homes. The missionary effort was launched, and the mother church was left to "rest," in much the same way a new birth mother rests in the quiet of her maternity ward after a long labor. The mother church was still in the able hands of their experienced pastor. The pressure of an overcrowded building was taken off the church staff. It seemed that everyone settled back into a more "comfortable" pace. Two years later, their pastor was promoted to a new position out of the area.

After interviewing many qualified candidates, the committee finally chose a replacement, and the congregation eagerly anticipated the arrival of their new pastor. Max's congregation was glad that the changing of the guard would be immediate and that the church would continue to be there for them, feeding them spiritually whenever they chose to attend. However, instead of continued peace and comfort, the next three years evolved into a snafu of unprepared pastors, political infighting, and a steady loss of membership. The church churned through a new pastoral candidate every six to eight months, until attendance was one-third of what it had been just a few years prior.

Three long years of frustration and disappointment went by, and the assembly still did not have a senior pastor. Slowly, the members of the congregation began to realize that the responsibility for the church's work rested on their own shoulders. Each member, individually and collectively, made up the "church." They were responsible for ministry. It was not just the pastor's job. Lay leaders began to step forward and take on new areas of responsibility. New adult classes began, and a renewed interest in the children's Sunday-school program was ignited. In short, each member stopped attending church and decided once again to be the church.

At that point God responded to their prayers and brought a mature pastor to the church who had a heart for evangelism and discipleship. Today this congregation is again reaching out into the community. They provide ministries to their inner-city children and have partnered with a local school to give the children backpacks filled with school supplies. The church has a training center for those looking to enter ministry, and they hold neighborhood events all year long as a means to reach the neighborhood families.

God's faithfulness and glory is what He desires to reveal in and through your life and in the life of His church. The blessings that come to us along the way are meant to facilitate that end, glorifying God. Just like what occurred in the climax of Joseph's life, when Max's church was ready to accept the responsibility of living like God's people, God reaffirmed His faithfulness and provided a leader who would build His kingdom, through which He could reveal His glory.

Take a minute and consider your life's current events, in your church, your family, your home, or with your parents or your children. In what ways would God want to glorify Himself through you in these circumstances? Maybe you hold a dream or a deeply held spiritual desire that is stalled on its path to fulfillment. Did you ever feel called to a particular type of ministry? Do you hold the seed of a divine promise in your heart, something you are now just waiting to see fulfilled?

Write your thoughts below.

_____

_____

_____

_____

_____

What about the prayers you have lifted to heaven that have not yet been answered? In what ways has God revealed to you that He wants to work through your life? Often a strong desire in your heart is the beginning of God's plan for you.

Write your thoughts below.

_____

_____

_____

_____

_____

Day Four: Heaven Waits on Earth

Joseph's life taught him that "right living" didn't always guarantee that good things would come immediately into his life. He also learned that even when the control of events was completely out of his own hands, right living is in itself a reward. Eventually, because God is faithful to His promises, God's blessing will come. But as for the timetable you may be expecting, and the timetable on which God is working…well, as God demonstrated in Joseph's life, they may be altogether different.

In a created universe governed by a loving God and the free will He gave to men, heaven often waits on earth. God waits for His people to take on His concerns, His character, and His heart before His lessons are learned and He blesses them. God's ways are so completely different from our own. In our cultural consumer mentality, we are used to getting whatever we want, whenever we want it. We can drive up to a restaurant, sit down to a gourmet meal, and pay for it with a plastic card. No mess, no fuss, and no cleanup; we simply insert our card and immediately receive whatever we want. In today's American church, this same mentality has encroached into our pulpits, and into our prayer life. I am told that when I pray and believe that I will receive, God is obligated to give me what I want. Right? A house, a job, a car — nothing is out of the realm of God's provision.

What would Joseph have thought of this kind of message as he sat in the prison cell? What would Jesus have thought of this message as He prayed in the Garden of Gethsemane? Jesus pleaded three times for God to let the cup of suffering, His death on the cross, pass Him by. He knew the anguish that lay before Him; yet His final prayer was, "Not My will, Father, but Yours be done."

Heaven waits on earth. Because God is a loving God, and we are His children, He does provide the things that we need. But there comes a time when our loving Father says no to the things we ask for because He is waiting for us to look deeper into His heart and discover that He holds a greater gift. Instead of giving us items that are temporal, that will perish, God wants to give us a greater revelation of Himself. This is a gift that will never fade; one that will change us forever. God has a perfect will — and that is for His children to grow up and be like Him. But because of His great love, God will not force His perfect will on our free will. And so, heaven waits on earth.

In Joseph's life, God personally forged circumstances in order to mold in Joseph's heart a reflection of His own. Joseph could have chosen to reject the character he had been taught as a little boy. He could have submitted to the world's pressure and taken on the character and image of any other slave. But he had a vision of another future — a different future that included the plans God had for him.

These lessons from Joseph's life were not instantly learned. He couldn't insert a credit card into God's slot machine and immediately arrive at a more comfortable place in his life. He was tested, tried, and proven over twenty-three years. Following his ordeal, Joseph had proven he could be trusted to rise to power. Let's push the pause button for a minute and consider a different Joseph. What if Joseph hadn't become a benevolent leader? What if he had continued to harbor bitterness and unforgiveness in his heart toward his brothers? When they walked through the palace gates that hot desert afternoon, if Joseph had not moved beyond his own bitterness, he could have ended God's plan. His brothers could have died in prison, or his whole family could have starved, if Joseph had decided to retaliate for what they had done to him those many years before. Then what would have happened to God's plan for the salvation of His people?

What do you think?

_____

_____

_____

_____

_____

_____

_____

Pondering these questions may seem a bit like wasted effort, because we know how the story turned out. But by considering Joseph and the choices he made, you can build a bridge into your life and to the choices you may face today.

Your story is not complete the way that Joseph's is. How can you further God's work in your life?

_____

_____

_____

_____

_____

What might be the ending to your story that you cannot see at this time?

_____

_____

_____

Joseph was given a dream early in his life that God fulfilled when Joseph was ready. Do you hold a dream or vision of the kind of Christian influence you hope to be — in your family, neighborhood, or city? Write the details of your spiritual aspirations below.

_____

_____

_____

_____

_____

Jesus identified certain specific steps that you could, and should, be taking if you want God's character to be formed in you. These are not legalistic "rules" that, when followed, will guarantee blessing and spiritual maturity. But these "divine suggestions" will lead you toward the fulfillment of the promises of God and the answers to the prayers that you have lifted up to heaven. These were lessons that Jesus taught by His example and backed up with His words. These steps may include, but aren't limited to:

Restoring a broken relationship
Read Matthew 18:15-19.

Regular fasting and prayer
Read Matthew 6:16-18 and Isaiah 58:6-9a.

Getting involved in a discipleship or accountability group
Read Acts 2:43-47 and 2 Timothy 2:2.

Forgiving someone who causes you harm
Read Matthew 6:12-15 and 18:21-35.

Writing a letter of encouragement to your pastor
Read 1 Thessalonians 5:11.

Establishing the discipline of daily prayer and Bible study time
Read Mark 1:35 and Acts 6:2-4.

Prayerfully consider these suggestions, and then make a list of three specific activities on which you will follow through. These steps will move you toward voluntarily surrendering your will to God and to what He is doing in your life.

1._____

2._____

3._____

Now take a look at your list. Is there anything that is directly preventing you from pursuing these options today? If a relationship is the issue, decide now to take the appropriate steps toward forgiveness so that you can move forward. If your desire is ministry, maybe it's time to look into your training. Does your church offer the schooling, support, and training that will take you toward fulfilling your dreams? What steps can you take to pursue your vision?

Each event in Joseph's life required his faithfulness. God was at work, and He is always at work around you, but He will not complete His will on His own. He looks for you to join Him in His work. It is your responsibility to partner with God and bring Him the glory.

Consider what your responsibility may be in fulfilling your dreams with God. Be practical, specific, and measurable. For example, a goal that is vague, such as, "Spend more time reading my Bible," is not a *specific* and *measurable* goal. A goal such as, "I will get up twenty minutes earlier in the morning to spend time praying and reading two chapters from the

Bible, starting with the gospel of John," is a specific, measurable goal that is much more likely to become a part of your daily routine.

List your specific, measurable goals below.

_____

_____

_____

_____

Finally, write a prayer to God, asking Him to help you carry out the goals that you have set.

_____

_____

_____

_____

_____

_____

Day Five: God Fulfills Dreams As We Are Faithful

As Joseph lived through the purifying tests that God set before him, he was changed. He became more like the God and the father whom he sought to honor by his behavior and his choices. After his period of testing was completed, he was released into expanded influence to lead the Egyptian nation as they prepared for the famine, and to administer the food reserves during the famine. The wisdom that was learned in the desert, the dungeon, and the darkness, brought blessing to Egypt, as well as God's chosen people, and through them, to the entire world.

In another story in the New Testament, God followed the same process to create a servant-leader's heart in another Christian's life. In the book of Acts, the apostle Paul changed from a vigorous persecutor of the church to a "super preacher" in the course of just a few short days. Look at the timeline of his conversion:

He stood in approval at Stephen's death.
Read Acts 8:1.

He persecuted the church.
Read Acts 8:1-3.

Suddenly, he was knocked off of his horse on the road to Damascus.
Read Acts 9:3-6.

Three days later he was converted and baptized.
Read Acts 9:9-19.

Immediately, he began preaching.
Read Acts 9:20-22.

What we do not see without a closer look into the history of the New Testament is that between his initial foray into street preaching, and the time that he was called by the Holy

Spirit and released into his first missionary journey, Paul settled in Antioch and grew in his faith for twelve to fourteen years. From the time of his conversion on the road to Damascus, to the beginning of Acts 13 (in which Paul and Barnabas were set apart for their first missionary journey), Paul spent time in Arabia, Damascus, Tarsus, and finally Antioch as his faith, relationships with the church, and revelation of the grace of God through Jesus Christ grew. He learned the ways of grace. He learned from the other disciples about the One he had persecuted. Like Joseph and David, Paul went through a period of maturing, testing, and building relationships in the body of Christ before God released him into ministry. But once that preparation was complete, God opened the doors, and the church learned to see God through the words and lessons of Paul's life.

Have you experienced a similar time of growth and preparation in your walk with God? Explain.

_____

_____

_____

_____

As with Joseph and David, there are times during the pruning process that emotional turmoil or trying circumstances can cloud your vision of God's purposes. The only tangible thing you may have to hold on to is your faith in a loving God. Hold on to what you know to be true: that God is your Provider, Protector, Father, Shepherd, and Guide, and then release Him to work in your life's circumstances. Release His hands to shape and form your heart by giving you a deeper revelation of Himself.

There are many promises in the New Testament that identify reasons why God may not answer our prayers. While our study so far has focused on the unseen ways in which God may be working in your life to shape your character for His ultimate plan for you, there may be other areas on which you need to focus.

The following list includes choices you may be making that can withhold God's blessing on your life.

Look up the following verses, and consider the promises and conditions on those promises — the choice that God places within your hands.

Psalm 138:6; James 4:6

What is the promise? _____

What is the condition? _____

What will you do in response? _____

Isaiah 59:1-2; 1 John 1:5-9

What is the promise? _____

What is the condition? _____

What will you do in response? _____

Psalm 66:18

What is the promise? _____

What is the condition? _____

What will you do in response? _____

Matthew 6:12-15

What is the promise? _____

What is the condition? _____

What will you do in response? _____

James 4:3

What is the promise? _____

What is the condition? _____

What will you do in response? _____

Zechariah 7:13; Romans 8:1-8

What is the promise? _____

What is the condition? _____

What will you do in response? _____

Matthew 6:33; Isaiah 29:13

What is the promise? _____

What is the condition? _____

What will you do in response? _____

Our God does not change. We do not come to Him on the basis of our own goodness, but we only are able to approach Him because of His grace. But God does expect that His grace will make an impact on our lives, and that we will begin to take on the nature and character of His Son.

Write out Titus 2:11-12.

_____

_____

_____

What should we do as a result of God's grace?

_____

_____

_____

_____

Let's return to the promises God has given you and the prayers you have raised up to Him. You've made your goal to glorify God in every circumstance. You've prayed about your situation. And you are acting in obedience to what you know He has told you to do. God's Word promises that He will meet you at that point. If your ideas are not in His will for you, as you begin to take action, He will redirect your efforts. But one thing is true, God cannot lead a stationary object. You can't steer a car that is sitting in your driveway. You have to be on the road — with the engine running, the fuel tank full of gas, the oil changed, and the tires checked — and be in motion on the road before you can guide your vehicle in a new direction.

God will take your life as you offer it to Him. Just as with Joseph, the God of the heavens will shape your life so He can fulfill the spiritual visions that He has given you. God opposes the proud, but through a person with a broken spirit and a contrite heart He will work miracles, especially when He knows you will be faithful to give Him glory for what He has done.

Father,

It is Your mercy and truth that uphold me and give me the courage to pursue Your image in my life. When I fall, please pick me up. When I triumph, help me remember that it is because of Your presence in my life that I can succeed. God, you have given me exceedingly great and precious promises through Your Word. Help me today to remain faithful to You so that I will see these promises come to pass and bring You glory. Help me act on those things that I know I can and should do. In Jesus' name I pray. Amen.

Week Seven: Summary

The king's heart is in the hand of the LORD; he directs it like a watercourse wherever he pleases. All a man's ways seem right to him, but the LORD weighs the heart. To do what is right and just is more acceptable to th LORD than sacrifice.

—Proverbs 21:1-3

This week's lessons have introduced you to some new ideas about Joseph and the ways in which God worked in his life. What is one new idea that you have learned this week? If there is one thought or idea that God used to grab your attention, write it on the lines below.

_____

_____

_____

_____

_____

_____

_____

_____

_____

Joseph

Simeon's Dream

A diamond shines brightest
when it's displayed from a
black velvet cloth.
In the same way,
God's love shines most clearly when
He cuts through the blackness
of our trying circumstances.

Day One: Take a Look at God's Word

When Joseph's brothers returned to their father, Joseph selected his brother Simeon to remain behind in jail. He wanted to test his brothers to see if the years had softened them or if they had remained the hardened, self-seeking bullies he remembered as a child. If Joseph's motives had been anger or revenge, he would have put them all in jail, or perhaps let just one return to his father. But Joseph's heart had been changed. His character had been molded by God during his time in Egyptian bondage, as would his ancestors' during the next 400 years.

There are questions that remain unanswered by Scripture in the account of Joseph's life. What happened in Jacob's tents during the almost thirty years between the time Joseph disappeared into the desert and when he was reunited with his family? What changes occurred in the family who would eventually be known as "God's chosen people"? As we began looking at the life of Joseph, we discovered a dysfunctional family. Each person was intent on harming the others in order to promote their own personal agendas. This does not reflect a character that God can bless, nor does it show the heart attitude that must be in place in the people whom God had chosen to be the foundation of His redemptive work for all mankind.

This week, we will examine Genesis 43-45. As you read these chapters, imagine that you are one of Joseph's brothers. What would you be thinking as the events unfolded around you? How would you have addressed the guilt for selling your own brother into slavery thirty years before, especially after it seems a ghost has returned to remind you of that very event? How would you respond as you returned to your father, Jacob, without one of your brothers? What thoughts would be filling your mind as you ran out of food — as you ate the last of the grain from the first trip to Egypt — knowing that in order to avoid starvation for you and your family, you would be forced to return to Egypt and face the man who had treated you so harshly?

Read Genesis 43 through 45, and record your thoughts on the lines below.

_____

_____

_____

_____

_____

While God has a perfect plan for our lives, He does not remove our feelings, emotions, hopes, or dreams as He draws us closer to Himself. It is often through the conflict between our feelings and the plan we sense in God's loving purposes that the greatest growth occurs in our lives.

In our study tomorrow, we will live these events through the perspective of one of Joseph's siblings, and begin to understand more deeply how God can bring His triumph out of our failures.

Day Two: Through Simeon's Weary Eyes

Joy lit Jacob's face as he looked up to see his sons returning from the fields in time for the evening meal. The cooling desert was a peaceful place, and Jacob looked forward to this time of community with his sons.

"Father, isn't this your son Joseph's coat?" one of them asked tersely. "We found it on the trail coming home." The joy in Jacob's face melted into sorrow like wax dripping down the side of a candle. Then he fell into a pool of anguished sobs as he realized the blood-covered tunic they held belonged to his favorite son. As Simeon watched his father's face, he saw that every muscle was contorted in pain. Tears rolled from Jacob's eyes into the depths of his soul as he fell to the ground and wept for Joseph. His favorite son was dead.

Simeon jerked awake, and the black darkness of his jail cell collapsed in on him again. The memory of his father's sobs echoed in the acrid darkness. His father had wept for days...no...months. The words now rang in Simeon's ears: "Isn't this your son's coat?" His coldheartedness toward both his father and brother did not allow him to ask, "Is this our brother's coat?" No, they thought of Joseph with disdain and had wished that he were not a part of the family for a very long time. But now, the memory of his cold words was matched only by the cold sweat that ran down the small of his back.

Simeon and his brothers had held their father in nearly as much contempt as they demonstrated toward their now-missing brother. The way he had favored Joseph and his mother, Rachel, made their blood boil. Simeon and the other sons of Leah had been the ones who built the family homestead. They had worked with their father herding sheep, spending hot days in the fields planting, and cold nights birthing lambs in the spring. By the sweat of their brows, they had earned the love that Jacob so carelessly bestowed on Joseph. But then, as the backlash of their anger toward their brother came to bear on their father, the brothers began to realize that they were the ones who had brought this pain into Jacob's life. They had brought irreversible pain in the life of the one who had given them life, inflicting an ordeal on Jacob from which he would never recover.

Simeon sat alone in the darkness of the Egyptian jail cell. He and his brothers had met with the Egyptian overlord upon their arrival to buy food, only to be rejected, accused of being spies, and corporately thrown in jail. Now Simeon remained behind as his brothers returned home. How long had it been…days…weeks…months? Simeon couldn't remember how many times he had seen the sun slipping past the small window above his stone mattress. But in the countless dark nights, his father singularly occupied his mind. From the moment his brothers had brought Joseph's blood-soaked tunic to the family tent, his father had never recuperated. Simeon pulled his knees to his chest as if to fight off the darkness. He cowered in the putrid inky blackness, remembering his father's mourning. In the following months, Jacob had elusively sought peace, but found no closure from the tragic events that had ripped open his heart.

Simeon remembered how Jacob's sorrow slowly turned to hostility over the next months, and then outright anger. As he wondered why God had taken his favorite son, this anger found a lightning rod in the lives of his other sons. The brothers had lacked any genuine unity, and their mothers' incessant wrangling fueled their own competitive animosity. Reuben, Simeon, Levi, Judah, Issachar, and Zebulon, although the largest group of siblings from Jacob's first wife, were never touched by the love their father showed to Rachel or her sons, Joseph and Benjamin. Then there were the handmaiden's sons, Dan and Naphtali. These were Simeon's half-brothers. They were part of the family…part of the clan…but they lived as if they were their own tribe, establishing their own tents and herds. Gad and Asher, Leah's handmaiden's sons, were born to the joy of their mother, but the oldest brothers had never shared her feelings. The coldness between the family sects separated them all, but became an accepted part of their family life.

This coldness now haunted Simeon again in the Egyptian jail cell. He was drenched in cold sweat and shivered uncontrollably as he fought with his conscience once more. What could he have done differently? Over the years the single meal shared among his brothers was the cold cup of bitterness toward each other. But as the reality of the pain they caused their father began to sink in, Simeon wished that they had been more forgiving.

These thoughts gnawed at Simeon's mind until he lay exhausted on his stone cot. The remainder of his energy was spent shooing rats away from his feet and fighting them for the bread and water that was shoved under the door. Try as he might, Simeon could not get off of the spinning potter's wheel whirling through his mind…his family, his brothers, his home. He wondered if his brothers would ever return to Egypt and retrieve him. Possibly Joseph's fate would become his own.

Eventually the sun poured into the window above his bed yet again. He stood on the stone slab, only to see the same merchant's feet and vendors selling their wares in the courtyard outside the king's gate. Alone in the cell, the sun and fresh air were his only companions. At the far end of the courtyard, he could just barely view a stage where he had seen the Pharaoh's overlord reading proclamations to the people.

Simeon slumped back down on his stone bed and again thought of Joseph…wondering if he were still alive. Again and again he replayed the conversations between him and his brothers as they tended sheep those thirty years. Their father had teetered from sorrow to hostility as he struggled with his loss, and the brothers' treatment of each other began to follow Jacob's example. The rejection they felt from Jacob as he pulled into his own grief, they threw at one another. Each brother took his flocks to his own corner of the region and argued about who would come to the well first. As their herds and flocks grew in number, so did the family wealth, which should have provided peace and security. But instead, sorrow and strife in the family never left their fields.

Simeon was the first to publicly acknowledge Jacob's agony and how he and his brothers had brought this pain upon themselves, but his brothers counted Simeon's reproof with icy contempt. They were unable to carry their father's anguish in addition to the guilt they shared. Simeon remembered nights around the campfire when Judah would chide them, asking why they had taken such a brash action. Reuben, the oldest, self-righteously repeated his plan to retrieve Joseph from the well after their anger had cooled. But then the Ishmaelites' caravan passed by…the wrong decision…the wrong time…and Joseph was gone for good.

Simeon began to wonder if his brothers would ever return. He vainly tried to squelch the fear that he would be forever abandoned, just as he had abandoned his brother Joseph. But the whispers in his mind continued — *his fate was simply justice for Joseph's betrayal, they said. The whole family would perish, because of one foolish decision.*

Simeon wrestled with these thoughts night after night, tossing and turning on the stone bed, his joints aching from lying on a cold slab. Each night he awoke to the same nightmare: Joseph's coat, stained with goat's blood, and the anguish on his father's face.

From our perspective, it is easy to question if Simeon's ordeal was necessary. This entire step in the process of reuniting Joseph and his family could have been avoided. Joseph could have revealed himself to his brothers the first time they wandered into the palace hall, but he didn't.

Why do you think Joseph responded this way?

_____

_____

_____

When God does a work in your life, before He releases you into an increased level of influence, He will test you. Before Joseph could bless his family, he decided to test them as well, to see if the events that had changed his life had brought any changes to his wayward family. What if his brothers had not returned to Egypt, but instead had left Simeon to die in jail? Joseph was willing to take that risk because he genuinely sought God's hand at work in his siblings' lives. He had learned the lessons of the desert and the dungeon well. Joseph knew that what was inside of a man determined his identity, and he wanted to see his brothers become men of character as well. And that leads us to the next principle in our study:

Principle Eight: After learning the lessons of mercy and justice, we may still see difficulty in the lives of those we love, as God works to build the same character in their lives as He built in ours.

How have you seen this principle take place in your own life?

_____

_____

_____

_____

_____

Day Three: Two Enduring Lessons from the Dungeon

In Jacob's house, as is true in every household, the character of the father was transferred to his sons. Jacob had been a conniving manipulator who thought nothing of favoring one family member over another, regardless of the pain it brought to those less preferred. Perhaps from our sheltered distance of history, we can say that God was dispensing some measure of justice on Jacob through the painful losses of his sons and wife. But it could be dangerous to be so self-righteous. In this mire of humanity, God was preparing for His own divine purposes to be fulfilled in Jacob's life, a fulfillment that would become His chosen people's heritage. God chose Jacob over Esau, and chose Jacob's sons to build Himself the Israelite nation. God chose to ultimately reveal Himself, first through this family, later through the covenant at Mt. Sinai, and finally through Jesus Christ.

What happens when someone is in the depth of pain…Joseph in the dungeon after the butler forgot him…his brothers as they left Egypt without Simeon? How can a person reach out and get a handle on God's grace and mercy in the midst of their difficulty? There are two distinct lessons that we can glean from the climax of this story:

Lesson One: God's purpose is not your pain.

The Bible says that *God opposes the proud but gives grace to the humble* (James 4:6). At the beginning of the story, Jacob and his sons, including Joseph, would have qualified as the former. Joseph eventually grew into the latter. Through divinely orchestrated circumstances, God subdued the pride, the arrogance, and the manipulative lifestyle that had defined this family's history. God can transform a man's heart, one that is walled off by high towers of personal pride and selfishness, through the difficulty that we bring into our own lives. And after the tribulations, we become ready to accept His hand of mercy. As we stay faithful, He redeems us and brings us into our personal promised land.

Write out Romans 8:28.

_____

_____

What happens to those who love God?

_____

_____

To whose purposes are we called?

_____

_____

_____

This verse does not guarantee that all things that enter your life will be pleasant. But God promises that as we love Him and remain called, walking according to His purposes, He will work out the conclusion for His good. For Joseph, Jacob, and the rest of the family, this took over thirty years. As Simeon sat in jail, Jacob was eating the last few scraps of grain from the bottom of his sons' bags. The brothers wondered what they were going to eat next week. None of them could yet see God's hand of mercy that would be extended to them through Joseph. They could only wrestle with the weight of their own choices.

It is this process of wrestling between our own feelings and God's will that changes us. Ultimately, it is not the disruptive circumstances alone that change our heart. God does not find delight in the suffering of His people. But sometimes, when we demonstrate to God that we are not listening to His Word, He will allow a disruption into our lives in order to create a divine tension between our own selfishness and God's loving will. The impetus that changes us is the effect of the choices we make. Will we choose to be faithful to God and His will, or will we choose to bow to our own?

It's time to place the theoretical against reality.

In your own life, think of a past event, or maybe a current situation, in which you see God working in your life the way He did with Jacob and his family. Describe these events on the lines below.

_____

_____

_____

_____

_____

In a culture that prides itself on self-reliance and independence, it can be difficult to accept the idea that we might not be in total control of our lives. Remember as you consider this principle in God's heart-softening process that He does not find pleasure by allowing difficulty, but He desires us to turn to Him and find a deeper revelation of Him through any problem or situation that may come.

If the event you listed above is a present situation, what do you think God's purpose may be? If it is a past event, take a minute and thank God for the lessons of His grace you learned from His hands.

_____

_____

_____

_____

Lesson Two:
Mercy triumphs over judgment.

God seeks to mold your heart, and that of any person who wishes to be given the responsibility of showing His love to the world. In his second letter to Timothy, Paul instructed his young protégé regarding one of his responsibilities as a maturing Christian.

Write out 2 Timothy 2:2.

_____

_____

_____

_____

What was Timothy to do with the lessons he had learned?

_____

_____

_____

_____

This process can only take place through a heart that understands the necessity of justice, but also that in the end mercy triumphs over judgment. God's judgment is never final!

What do you think about the statement, "God's judgment is never final"? Have you ever seen this take place in your own life?

_____

_____

_____

In our American culture, we face many obstacles to accepting these lessons. Our success-based lifestyles can insulate us from the pain of failure. We shy away from situations in which we cannot be successful or we can't control the setting. We endeavor to control all of the variables so as to avoid failure and pain and manufacture success and comfort. So when God knocks at the door with an unexpected package of difficulty, we quickly slam it closed and latch the bolt. We are unaware that He desires to teach us some of the same lessons we see in Joseph's life.

A good friend of mine and his wife ran a daycare in his home, and he told me this story. His wife loved kids, and each day, at snack time, Marge brought out a tray of fruit. One day, to Jim's dismay, the children were clamoring over who got to eat the black bananas. The children didn't want the bright yellow ones; they fought over who would receive the black, mushy fruit! After the kids were gone for the day, Jim pulled his wife aside and asked her to explain the unusual events. Marge interpreted the odd spectacle this way. Earlier that day, she had explained to the children that the "blackness" in the peel was only the sugar showing itself, so the black bananas were actually the sweetest ones of the bunch. She looked at Jim and smiled. "It's all a matter of perspective!" If you could see every event in your life from God's perspective, the most difficult situation would appear to be no more troublesome than a passing rain cloud.

So the question is, when difficulty enters your life, how will you respond? You can blame others and make excuses for your own behavior, or you can surrender to what God is trying to do in your life.

God leaves the choice of how you respond up to you. How do you tend to respond to the "gift" of tribulation?

_____

_____

_____

For Simeon, he didn't have any choices left. Everything had to be stripped away from him and his brothers before they were willing to confront their own corrupt hearts. Difficulty often has a facet of uncontrollability attached to it. Just as Simeon finally relinquished his hopes and dreams in the darkness of his despair, so God asks you to surrender to your situation, look up to heaven, and remember the goodness of God's provision, on His terms.

As you pause to consider this lesson, think of the event you listed above. How did you respond? If it is a current event, have you surrendered to God, and looked for His will in the midst of the situation? If not, make your entry below a prayer of surrender and thanksgiving.

_____

_____

_____

_____

_____

_____

These are some of the lessons that can soften your heart. Whatever the purpose of the pain, whatever the purpose of the difficulty, the God we serve is not a God who delights in His people's suffering. God delights in the salvation of His people. He wants to bless us, but sometimes that blessing, which is a further revelation of Himself, comes from lessons we learn through difficulty.

Day Four: The Purpose Is Love

Joseph's response to his brothers' audience demonstrates the extent of his love. He had learned to love through his ordeal. So when his brothers returned to their father's house, Joseph returned their gold in each one of their bags. He yearned to bless his family. His heart ached to rejoin his father, brothers, and the rest of the family. But in the shifting circumstances and the process of God's unfolding will, Joseph needed to know that the blessings he desired to pour out on his family would be accepted.

Although he created some of the difficulties in his brothers' lives, Joseph paints an example of our Savior whose greatest desire is to bless our lives. God wants to bless you by drawing you to Himself. But He insists that you allow Him to change your heart first so that you can fully experience the blessings He desires to bestow.

The story of Jacob, Joseph, and his brothers demonstrates God's masterpiece of grace and shows how mercy triumphs over pain. It clearly illustrates God's divine heart-changing process. God's purpose in each step was to reveal His love, first to Joseph, and then *through* Joseph to his family. The climax of this story explodes with unrestrained love as Joseph finally reveals himself to his brothers and declares, "What you meant for evil, God intended for good!"

Reread Genesis 45:1-5.

How did Joseph demonstrate forgiveness?

_____

_____

_____

In what ways did he become the provider for his family?

_____

_____

_____

How did Joseph recognize God's hand in all that had happened?

_____

_____

Now read Genesis 50:15-21.

Why were Joseph's brothers afraid of him?

_____

_____

How did Joseph respond?

_____

_____

What was God's final purpose in this situation?

_____

_____

This is a picture of the love and plans God has for you. His purpose in allowing trials or difficulty into your life is not to squash you into submission so that eventually you will give up and follow Him. No, the purpose is to reveal that in all things, in life and death, in darkness and triumph, in hope and despair, He remains right beside you. His love for you crosses all boundaries. Even when the trying events of your life are the rightful consequences of your own choices, God holds out His loving hand, inviting you to turn from sinful choices and receive His love again.

Joseph engineered the circumstances in his family's life so that if they had truly let go of their bitterness, they would appear before him again. Just as the dungeon was a test of Joseph's integrity, the gold Joseph put in the tops of his brothers' sacks was a test of their honesty. Would they return for more grain? If so, would they reveal the returned gold that Joseph had placed in their bags? If they came back, but kept the gold, what would that have said about their hearts, their integrity?

Pause and consider the events from your own life you have described during this week's lessons. What are the lessons God has taught or is teaching you right now?

Are you still stuck in the dungeon? Are you in a place where God is testing the lesson? Or have you learned to soften your heart and been placed in a position to pass the lessons on to others?

_____

_____

_____

_____

_____

Write out 2 Chronicles 7:14.

_____

_____

_____

_____

This verse was a promise given to Solomon at the dedication of the great temple in Jerusalem, and it describes God's efforts to initiate a close relationship with His people.

How does this verse demonstrate the lessons we have learned this week from Joseph's life?

_____

_____

_____

_____

_____

Isn't it the same process? When Joseph's heart was humbled and God's time was perfect, the situation changed. As you draw near to God, you will be tested — not to prove yourself to an all-knowing and almighty God, but to learn the habits that will allow God to release His love into your life in unfathomable ways. The ultimate purpose is love — God's love for you — so that you will have a prepared heart that can receive everything He has for you.

In the final minutes of today's study, write out these three familiar Bible passages, and let them seep deep into your mind and heart as you consider everything God has done in your life.

Write out Romans 8:28-39.

_____

_____

_____

_____

_____

_____

_____

_____

_____

What meaning does this passage have for you?

_____

_____

_____

Write out Ephesians 3:14-19.

_____

_____

_____

_____

_____

_____

_____

What meaning does this passage have for you?

_____

_____

_____

_____

_____

_____

_____

_____

Write out 2 Corinthians 5:14-20.

_____

_____

_____

_____

_____

_____

_____

What meaning does this passage have for you?

_____

_____

_____

_____

_____

_____

_____

_____

Day Five: Loving and Leading

Picture a flashlight, turned on and setting bulb-side down on a table in a darkened room. All that is visible is a small ring of light showing through the plastic collar. The plastic hides any more of the beam than this from illuminating the room. If the flashlight is lifted slightly, the white light jumps from the lens and casts its bright white glow onto the table. As the light is lifted farther, the circle of light expands, transforming more of the dark room by its brilliance.

The influence you can have on others is much like the beam from that flashlight. The more your life is elevated, the more light you can cast on the world around you. It is God who ultimately elevates a person into influence, leadership, or ministry. Although we might prefer to ignore the lessons from Joseph and David, allowing God to adjust our character through difficulty is a part of His plan. James puts it this way:

> *Consider it pure joy, my brothers, whenever you face trials of many kinds, because you know that the testing of your faith develops perseverance. Perseverance must finish its work so that you may be mature and complete, not lacking anything.*
>
> —James 1:2-4

After learning the lessons of God's faithfulness and allowing God's character to be imprinted on your heart, you are then given the responsibility of an expanded level of influence, to lead others along the same path. Did God raise up Saul and transform him into the apostle Paul, just so he could sit in a church and enjoy the teaching? Did Jesus forgive Peter's betrayal so that Peter could stay in the Upper Room and pray? The answer to these questions is a resounding no! The blessings, gifts, and callings that God has given you are for the express purpose that you will *give to others* and lead them to a relationship with the living God!

Write out Ephesians 2:10.

_____

_____

_____

Before the foundation of the world, God's plans included creating and loving you. From the day He measured out the waters and separated them from the land, He knew that His Son would die on a cross in order to communicate that love. And from the moment He lit the first star to give light in the blackness of the night, God desired that His love would be communicated through you to the other people in your life. Some call this process "evangelism;" others call it "setting a good example." Some call it "discipleship;" still others call it simply "living for Jesus with all of your heart." By whatever label, the Great Commission we accept as believers is to lead others to Christ so that they too can experience His love.

Look at the ways in which you are a leader. Maybe you're a leader to your children. Maybe you're a leader in your place of work, managing other people's time and talents. If you're still in school, maybe you are a leader on a sports team or in a club. You could simply be in a place of influence among your peers. But you have been given the truth about God's love, God's will for people's lives, and the sin that separates people from Him.

God holds you accountable, as a leader and as an influencer of people, to teach those whom you lead about His love.

Think about those over whom you have influence, and then read Romans 13:1. From where does all leadership and authority come?

_____

_____

_____

God has placed you as an influencer exactly where He wants you to be.

In what ways are you a leader and an influencer of others?

_____

_____

_____

_____

_____

_____

What are some of the ways you can be a *godly* leader, accountable and obedient to God for what He has taught you?

_____

_____

_____

_____

_____

What are some of the struggles in leading others that you run into on a regular basis? They may be related to clashes of personality, of motives, or of desires. If you are a mother, this could be an obstinate two-year-old child who stomps his feet and says, "No!" to anything you ask. If you are a parent of a teenager, your leadership struggle could be that teenager's time of stretching his wings and testing his boundaries. He may just be discovering himself and his world, but he still needs guidance from you. Or an obstinate or difficult coworker could be the test of the lessons you've learned.

What are your personal challenges in godly leadership?

_____

_____

_____

_____

_____

Following the principles God has taught you and building those same principles into the lives of those whom you influence can be challenging, even difficult, and the process is often filled with conflicting emotions. After Joseph's initial meeting with his brothers, he chased them away and locked one of them in jail. Then he retreated to his own home and wept so loudly that the servants throughout the house could hear him. These brothers were the ones whom Joseph had longed to embrace; yet he knew that they were also going to go through a time of testing before he would be able to bless them in the way that he wanted.

Isn't this the challenge of parenting? Or of running a business? Today's desires must be balanced with tomorrow's needs. And all issues at stake must be weighed in the balance of God's principles and His love.

What do you believe are God's goals for you in your role as an influencer?

_____

_____

_____

_____

_____

_____

_____

_____

You may not be able to control others, but you can encourage them in the opportunity to learn and grow.

As we close our time spent focusing on lessons from the life of Joseph, spend a few quiet moments meditating on God's workings in your own life. Then write a prayer below, asking God to help you stay faithful to what He has taught you. Ask Him for help in bringing the revelation of His blessing to those over whom He has given you responsibility and leadership influence.

Write your prayer below.

_____

_____

_____

_____

_____

_____

When you pass on the lessons you have learned to others, they can pass the blessings of those lessons to even more people, and the Great Commission is being fulfilled. God calls us to build disciples in our homes, in our neighborhoods, in our places of work, in our families, and among our friends. Go forth into the world, making disciples of all nations, starting in Jerusalem, Judea, Samaria (your own neighborhood), and to the uttermost parts of the earth (out of your comfort zone). Will you accept God's call to fulfill the Great Commission in your life?

Write your response in the lines below.

_____

_____

_____

_____

_____

_____

_____

Father,

You know my heart, and You know all things about me. You know when I lie down, and when I awake in the morning. There are so many things You know about me that I don't know myself. When life gets difficult, I am tempted to give up and turn to my own ways of getting what I want. Father, the path I long to walk is the path that leads straight to You. Please help me see that You are in control, and that if I will be faithful to You, You will work all things together for the good. Thank You for Your love. In Jesus' name. Amen.

Week Eight: Summary

And I said, My strength and my hope is perished from the LORD: Remembering mine affliction and my misery, the wormwood and the gall. My soul hath them still in remembrance, and is humbled in me. This I recall to my mind, therefore have I hope. It is of the LORD's mercies that we are not consumed, because his compassions fail not. They are new every morning: great is thy faithfulness. The LORD is my portion, saith my soul; therefore will I hope in him.

—Lamentations 3:18-24 KJV

This lesson has completed our study of Joseph, and the way God worked in his life. If there is one insight or idea which summarizes what you have learned so far, write it on the lines below.

_____

_____

_____

_____

_____

_____

_____

_____

Next week, in the final section of our study, we will turn to Israel's kings Saul and Hezekiah, two influencers who did not live the examples of faithfulness you've seen in Joseph and David. These kings allowed the selfish habits that infected their hearts to control their choices and ultimately separate them from God's purposes. You will discover how to draw closer to God's heart by learning to avoid their mistakes.

SECTION THREE
Kings Saul & Hezekiah

Introduction to Section Three

The series of events God uses to change hearts transformed David and Joseph into godly men who put God's desires ahead of their own. This divinely orchestrated inner transformation was reinforced by David and Joseph's personal choices. Without personal choice that engages the heart and will, serving God becomes legalistic, something that is forced upon us by rules and regulations. The transforming power of God's love can be muted by legalism, diminished by the expectation that God's response is limited to our own ability to keep the law.

The true love of God transforms you, and it is totally unconditional — not based on anything you have done, or will do. God's love cannot be bought, coerced, or forced, but you do have a choice as to how you will respond. Will you follow God's will or travel a path that follows your own desires?

The Israelites were repeatedly encouraged to trust God with all of their hearts. God sent numerous prophets and preachers to make them aware of the worldly influences that could slowly cool their heart's flame for their Maker.

Mixing a life that is devoted to God with your own self-serving motives is much like putting salt in a tall glass of iced tea. The salt may look exactly like sugar. It dissolves in the drink just like sugar does. But the resulting beverage is an unpalatable disappointment on a hot summer day. A life of divided interests is equally disappointing to a loving God. He desires that your life be lived to the fullest through your complete surrender to Him.

Kings Saul and Hezekiah are not remembered with the same veneration as are Joseph or David. These two kings did not learn that following God was first a matter of the heart. In this third and final section, we will discover that their deeds were a mixture of devotion, partial obedience, and decisions made out of fear and self-interest. Just like a mixture of iced tea and salt, Saul and Hezekiah left a disappointing legacy. They faltered under the pressures of life and left a wake of devastation in the lives of people whom they led. Just as David and Joseph's lives illustrated principles to a pure, devoted heart, from these men we will learn lessons built on the legacy of self-seeking motives. Let's learn how to avoid their mistakes, and begin to serve God with a completely devoted heart.

Saul

Fearing God or Fearing Man

God did not call us to be "trucemakers;" He called us to be peacemakers. And peace comes through overcoming, absolute victory.

—Ed Cole

Day One: Take a Look at God's Word

David and Joseph's lives demonstrated that a mere promotion to power doesn't prepare men to be leaders. God used the time prior to releasing His promises to them to prepare them to be godly men. They learned to lead with a character that reflected God's heart for His people. Someone once said, "As you grow in the Lord and have a sense of your calling and destiny, God brings you into situations that cause your character to catch up to your calling." During those times, we become transformed into men and women who honor God above all else.

Even Jesus was not immune to the divine character-building process that precedes release and blessing.

Write out Hebrews 5:8.

_____

_____

_____

_____

How did Jesus learn obedience?

_____

_____

_____

_____

So what is the key to becoming more like David, a man after God's own heart? So far, you have learned eight principles that God uses to purify the hearts of His people. If you will let Him, God will use these principles in subtle ways in your life, to change your selfish nature into a heart that is focused on pleasing Him. Beyond God's willingness to change you through these lessons, the answer is painfully simple. The outcome is up to you. It is up to you what kind of fruit will grow in your life. You can choose to walk a path that will cause you to experience everything that God has planned for you.

Look up Ephesians 3:20 and write it out on the lines below.

_____

_____

_____

How could this verse specifically apply to your life?

_____

_____

Look up Jeremiah 33:3, and write it out on the lines below.

_____

_____

_____

_____

_____

How could this verse specifically apply to your life?

_____

_____

Lastly, take a look at Jeremiah 29:11-13.

What does God have planned for you?

_____

_____

What is His promise to you?

_____

_____

What is the "condition," your part in seeing this promise fulfilled in your life?

_____

_____

_____

Instead of following God's path, you can follow your own will and selfish tendencies that turn away from all the great things that God desires to do in your life. Ultimately, the choice is in your hands every day.

This week's lesson seeks to answer the question, "Why don't more men and women grow into a relationship with God like that of David or Joseph?" The tragic consequences of King Saul's life grew out of his continual decisions to turn aside from God's plans. Saul first turned away from God in his heart, and then this heart attitude was reflected in his actions.

King Saul ruled over the fledgling Israelite nation before David came to power. As we have already seen in the first section of our study, a serious fault line ran through the center of Saul's life and created instability throughout his reign. From the heights of military success to the depths of foreboding depression, King Saul's instability was matched only by the depth of David's devotion to God.

The events of this week's story are recorded in 1 Samuel 15. As you read this passage, reflect on all of the details of this pivotal moment in the lives of Samuel, King Saul, and the entire Israelite nation.

Read 1 Samuel 15. As you consider this story, record your thoughts about Saul's choices, Samuel's involvement, and the action God took in Saul's life, on the lines below.

Saul's choices

_____

_____

Samuel's involvement

_____

_____

God's action

_____

_____

Day Two: God's Judgment of the Amalekites

This week, rather than moving straight into the narrative portion of our study, we will spend an additional day focusing on the historical setting of the events of 1 Samuel 15. Today's lesson will set up these remaining historical props and background scenery for the drama that is about to unfold.

Because the Amalekites play such an important role in our story, let's first look at who they were and how they related to God's people, Israel.

The Amalekites were a warring tribe that lived to the south of the Israelite kingdom. They coexisted in a turbulent relationship with God's people for generations. The Amalekites first opposed Israel during their exodus passage from Egypt to the Promised Land. As the exiled slave-nation traversed the desert toward the land of Jehovah's promise, the Amalekites came out in full force against them. When Moses and the children of Israel were about to pass into the Amalekite's territory (to the south), they humbly requested to walk through unopposed.

God's people had their own food and supplies, and they were on their way toward what would be Canaan, 180 miles to the north. But rather than bestowing permission, the Amalekites engaged Israel in battle. The Amalekites attacked the sick, feeble, and the elderly who lagged at the rear of the column. Although Israel fought back and won a mighty victory under Moses' intercessory hands, God never released Amalek from responsibility for their hostility. Forty years later, as the Israelite tribes stood ready to cross Jordan and enter Canaan, Moses recounted the memorable battle.

Write out Deuteronomy 25:19.

_____

_____

_____

_____

_____

This story of King Saul's war against the Amalekites is set more than 400 years after Israel crossed the Jordan River into the Promised Land. The Israelites had settled into their homeland and were now under Saul's leadership. Samuel sent word to Saul that it was time to strike the final blow against this enemy of Israel. The Amalekites, led by King Agag, once again were engaged against the Israelites in what should have been a final battle. Through the prophet Samuel, God issued instructions that would fulfill His word given in Deuteronomy 25. And God's instructions were very explicit. Saul was to destroy everything — the women, the children, the animals, the men, the warriors — everything was to be slaughtered before the outcome of this battle would be acceptable to God.

We are given no hint as to why a loving God would demand such a harsh punishment — other than the fact that it was to demonstrate His justice and to obliterate sin. But the purpose of this lesson is not to debate God's request. We must accept at face value that there was a purpose in His plan.

Running somewhat counter to God's commands were the typical military rules of the day: To the victor went the spoils, and after battle, the victorious army often spared the king's life in order to parade him as a trophy in their own land. Confiscating silver, gold, or livestock was also common, as this would increase the wealth of the victorious nation. So God's order for total annihilation was an unexpected aberration from the policies of a typical military campaign. Unfortunately, Saul's heart was not set on following God's commands. Other desires tugged at his heart, and his disobedience would haunt him throughout the rest of his reign as Israel's king.

In the light of this historical background, reread 1 Samuel 15. Write out God's request of Saul.

_____

_____

_____

_____

Why was God's request a fair and just one?

_____

_____

_____

Through his actions, what was Saul's reply?

_____

_____

Note Agag's response in verse 32. Why would this attitude have been repulsive to God?

_____

_____

What did Samuel do to fulfill God's request?

_____

_____

Why did Samuel grieve over Saul? (verse 35)

_____

_____

Take time with this last question. We often assume that God's desire to bless us and care for His people will always result in good things coming into our lives. While God's nature never changes, He brings both goodness and discipline into our lives. In light of the history between Israel and the Amalekites, God's commands, Saul's actions, and Samuel's response, how does God's severe judgment of Saul now appear to you?

_____

_____

_____

_____

_____

_____

_____

_____

_____

Day Three: To Obey Is Better Than Offering Sacrifices to God

The cool night slowly surrendered to the warm sunshine just outside of Jerusalem. As was his practice, Samuel rose to meet God in the early light. Today he was greeted by a lost lamb standing in his tent's entry.

"Baa-aa-aa." Samuel slowly rose from his cot. "Baa-aa-aa-aa!!" cried the insistent lamb.

O Lord, Samuel prayed, *this lost lamb greets me this morning. How many times have I risen to hear Your voice as the first sound in my ears? But today this lost sheep bleats to welcome me.*

Today I will rejoice with Saul over the victory over King Agag. On the plains of Omri we will praise You for Your victory. Samuel quieted himself as he prayed, and he thought over Saul's history as the king of Israel. *God, I remember meeting Saul on the plains as he searched for his father's donkeys. He was brash, handsome, and tall. I knew as he came over the hill that You had a special plan for him. He was so concerned with his father's lost animals, I was sure he would be a good shepherd over Your people.*

Samuel continued to pray and worship the Lord. He remembered the day of Saul's anointing to be king. Samuel knew who would be the king, but the people of Israel had not yet heard God's choice. So Samuel had separated them by tribes. They cast lots to the tribe of Benjamin, and then to the family of Kish. From this small family, Saul was set aside. *I called out for Saul, Lord, and he was nowhere to be found. I called again, and as we searched, his family found him among the boxes of supplies. He was hiding. I never quite understood King Saul that morning. Days earlier, when we met on the plains, I anointed him and showed him that he was to be the king. He prayed and prophesied for the entire day. Lord, Your Spirit came upon him in such a mighty way. Why was he hiding among the baggage when I called his name? Jehovah God, there are some things that this grey head will never understand.*

As Saul stood upright, he was head and shoulders above his brothers, a tall and handsome leader and a shepherd over Your people. Samuel continued to worship God and recount God's blessings upon King Saul's life. *Saul has been a warrior for Your people. Thank You, God, for Saul and the king he has become.* As Samuel bowed to worship, he realized that he had done most of the talking. Again, he quieted his heart and listened for the still, small voice of the most high God, the presence of the Almighty that he knew so well. He thought over the past years, to times when he had worshipped with King Saul. Samuel focused on God's throne, wanting to hear His heart this morning.

"Baa-aaa-aa-aa!"

"Be gone with you! Leave me alone with my God." The lamb cocked his head defiantly and stared at the prophet. He too was in need of a shepherd. Then God spoke to Samuel's heart.

This day I repent of having made Saul the king over Israel. You'll find Saul on the battlefield of disobedience. He did not follow My commands. This day I have rejected him as king over My people. Go meet with him. Speak to him the words that I will give you. Samuel rose, and the lamb at the door reluctantly scampered back to his flock. He donned his tunic and began his journey to meet the king. Samuel was troubled by the ominous sense of the Lord's displeasure that weighed upon his heart.

As Samuel traveled along the lonely path toward the fields and hills at Omri, a raven joined him, floating just ahead of the prophet on the warming morning breezes. He pondered this companion as it cawed to the warm sun. He remembered the day he had anointed Saul as Israel's king. God had displayed His displeasure that day over His people's desire for a ruler other than Himself. *Father God, my Provider, is this why You are unhappy with Saul today? Because of Your people's desire for a king?* The heavens above him remained eerily silent.

Father God, I know that Your people wanted a king because it was hard for them to understand You. They wanted a king so they could be like the nations around them. They needed security in the strength of horses and soldiers. Father God, You have been our security from the day we left Egypt. You have been the shield before and behind us. Lord, I know You were displeased with Your people that day. Will we return to the time of the judges? Will we return to a land without a king? Samuel's thoughts continued along this path as he journeyed, but he offered a sacrifice of praise that brought peace to his heart even though he didn't completely understand God's will. The heavens still watched silently, except for the call of the lonely raven drifting on the breezes just ahead of him.

As Samuel approached the battlefield from the south, evidence of the previous day's fury was strewn like chaff around a threshing floor. Remains of soldiers and their mounts filled the valley, amid abandoned arrows and swords. Samuel paused; he had to adjust himself to death's pungent smell drifting up from the canyon floor. As he picked his way down the steep hillside, Samuel spotted Saul's tent at the far end of the canyon.

From the fallen troops, broken equipment, and corpses scattered throughout the canyon, Samuel could see that King Saul had planned his attack well. Israel had scouted the Amalekite army's approach. Unaware of Israel's presence, the Amalekites traveled a road which crossed directly in front of the box canyon. The bulk of Israel's army hid themselves behind the hills to the north as Saul sent a small party as a ruse. Once spotted, they feigned retreat and led the Amalekites directly across the mouth of the canyon. As the Amalekites pursued Israel's decoy, the hidden troops attacked them from their flank. The ambush was successful, and Saul drove the Amalekites into the ravine from which there was no escape. They were slaughtered under the desert sun.

Samuel now realized that the raven was following the scent of the previous day's battle. The unclean carrion rode the breezes that carried the stench of death. Halfway through his descent down the hillside, Samuel paused to rest. The unsettling presence that he had felt from God that morning intensified as the specter of death engulfed him. Soldier's bodies covered acres of desert sand. Some of them still clenched their swords; others were pinned to the sand by their opponent's weaponry. *Jehovah, in life we are so different, but in death we are all the same. Lord, have mercy on us.* Silent prayers drifted from Samuel's mind to God's heart as he traversed the bloody desert floor. His progress was slow. Samuel had come to offer sacrifices with Saul, so he could not touch the dead, unclean bodies. It was difficult to walk without the tassels on his tunic skimming the corpses that littered the ground.

Samuel rounded a large heap of rocks and was startled by the now familiar raven. Settled atop a spear, the black bird cawed. The raven's hollow black eyes stared at the prophet as if it had been waiting for him.

"Sque-caaww-aaww." The bird's harsh call unsettled the old prophet. It was challenging Samuel, daring him to take its trophy. Poised arrogantly atop the end of an Amalekite spear, the bird claimed as its own the grotesque memorial of the prior day's battle. Under it lay two warriors, frozen in death's iron grasp.

The ominous shroud of death's reality covered Samuel as a cloak. He looked down to see the bottom of his robe covered in blood. There would be no sacrifice to Jehovah this day. But with the sense of foreboding surrounding him, Samuel no longer was in a presence of mind to offer praises to his God.

As he strode carefully across the last few hundred yards, Samuel thought back to the promises God had made to Abraham, the father of the Israelite people. Years before Abraham had received Isaac as a son, and centuries prior to the children of Israel's emigration from Egypt, God's promise was given — this land would be theirs, and God Himself would displace the tribes who had called the land home.

These were the only thoughts that brought Samuel a measure of peace as he ascended from the valley of death. God had known these battles would occur — and He knew the ultimate outcome. His purposes were good, even if Samuel didn't understand them. Samuel renewed his trust in God with these thoughts.

He trudged up the incline leading to Saul's tent, hearing the sounds of rejoicing that drifted in the breeze. The Israelite warriors were celebrating the previous day's battle. It had been a mighty victory for them. But death still weighed heavily on Samuel's heart. His encounter in the valley was now buttressed by the words of judgment and warning that Samuel had received from God earlier that morning.

At the top of the hill, just outside of Saul's field camp, Samuel was suddenly greeted by the sounds of the Amalekites' flocks. They bleated thanksgiving for their lives. To Samuel's further surprise, King Agag of the Amalekites was tied to a stake among the cattle and sheep. He smirked at the prophet as Samuel walked toward Saul's tent. Agag knew his troops' fate. Very few Amalekites, his son among them, had escaped the day. He was now confident that at least his own life would be spared as a ransom.

The bleating of the sheep alerted Saul, and he strode confidently out of his campaign headquarters to meet the prophet. "Samuel," Saul called out, "praise God! You're here to sacrifice with us. Jehovah has given us a mighty victory. I have obeyed Him just as you said, and I have brought this victory to the children of Israel."

Samuel stood quietly, stunned in disbelief with Saul's proclamation. The words rattled in his mind. "King Saul," the prophet replied after a moment of silence, "if you have obeyed the voice of the Lord, what is the bleating of sheep that I hear? And what are the spoils of war that I see the men dividing among themselves?"

Saul replied quickly as though he had not heard. Either he had forgotten God's command from days earlier, or he had changed it to suit his own purposes. "We obeyed the Lord and brought this mighty victory to Israel! We saved the best of the flocks to sacrifice. And Agag, we will bring him back as a testimony to the Lord's victory." Suddenly Samuel understood why the Lord had repented of making Saul king. The heart of Saul was not right with God. His obvious desire for personal aggrandizement displaced any hope that Samuel might have had that this king would be obedient to the One who had selected him.

With unction from God's Spirit, Samuel lowered his voice and asked, "Is the Lord so concerned with sacrifice as He is with your obedience to His voice? Saul, to obey is better than sacrifice, and to hearken to His Word is superior to the fat of the lambs on the temple altar."

Saul reeled under the impact of Samuel's words as if he had received a soldier's hammer blow to his breastplate. But it was the Spirit of God who chastised the king under the desert sun. As Samuel's words echoed across the plains, he locked his gaze into Saul's eyes and addressed the general who stood at the king's right hand. "Bring me a sword, and bring me King Agag." The general handed Samuel his own sword, then untied Agag from among the animals and led him directly to the prophet. His gaze still fastened to Saul's, Samuel reminded Agag how his people had opposed the living God and His people. Samuel recounted the history of Agag's tribe's opposition to the Israelites during their exodus, and how he had chosen a path of resistance to God's plan. Then, with one sudden slash of the sword, Agag joined his army in Sheol.

The king's head rolled across the sand and stopped at Saul's feet, frozen in a hideous expression of the fear that had filled Agag's final moments. Saul unlocked his eyes from Samuel's and gazed in astonishment at Agag's ghastly corpse in the sand. He finally comprehended the depth of his sin against God and began to tremble. Taking Samuel by the arm, he stepped out of earshot of his troops. "Samuel, please pray for me. I've done wrong in the sight of God. I feared the men who wanted to bring back some of the best spoils of victory. They wanted King Agag to be paraded through the streets. Please pray for me and sacrifice today with my men so that I will still have respect in their eyes."

Samuel had a difficult time restraining his disbelief as the shallowness of Saul's heart was revealed. He gazed directly into Saul's soul, and with the words that God had spoken that morning, Samuel replied, "This day God has taken the kingdom from you and given it to another. This day He is sorry that He made you the king over His people. On the day I met you on the plains, God gave you His Spirit. But He could not give you His heart, and yours is sorely lacking before Him this day. I will not sacrifice with you — nor will I see you ever again."

With these final words, Samuel turned to go. Saul fell to his knees one last time and reached for Samuel's cloak. He grasped a corner of Samuel's blood-stained tunic, and as the prophet turned, it tore off in Saul's hands.

Samuel wheeled, and considered the shell that this king had become, a hollow vestige of what the prophet had hoped Saul would be. "This day God has torn the kingdom from your hand and given it to another. To obey is better than sacrifice, Saul, and to listen to God's commands is better than the fat of rams. Remember this day, Saul. You will carry it to your grave." Samuel turned and descended back into the valley, walking slowly among the corpses and the ravens. The desert carrion birds' squawks masked the sound of Samuel's tears. He wept for his people. He wept for the fallen soldiers. He wept for the broken heart of God who had lost a king and a leader over His people that day.

Principle nine in God's process of heart transformation is revealed in this account of Saul's demise:

Principle Nine: Personal obedience to God is a cornerstone of our love relationship with Him. Partial obedience, delayed obedience, or altering God's requests to fit our own desires or lifestyle, is disobedience, and is irrefutable proof of a divided heart.

How is principle nine reflected in this account? In Saul's decisions? In Samuel's rebuke? Record your thoughts below.

_____

_____

_____

_____

_____

Day Four: Fearing God and Loving His Word

Obedience is not a popular topic in Christian circles today. Beyond a sermon or lesson on the Ten Commandments, it's rarely mentioned from our modern pulpits. It's so much more "refreshing" and "inspiring" to discuss topics such as love, salvation, and grace. But obedience is an important subject because when we obey God's commands, we are actually doing what is best both for ourselves and for His purposes in the earth.

As believers, we realize that our salvation is a gift, not something we have to earn. God does not keep a balance sheet in heaven, measuring our "good deeds" against our "bad deeds." Salvation was purchased in full by the death and resurrection of Jesus Christ.

Write out Ephesians 2:8-9.

_____

_____

_____

How have we been saved?

_____

_____

Why is it that no person can boast of their salvation?

_____

_____

Thank God that we cannot earn heaven! Could you imagine being in heaven with men and women who are constantly comparing their crowns to each other's to see which one of them did more "good works" while on the earth?

Imagine sitting in Café Manna, and the conversation going something like this: "You know, Jim, I think that George should only have one jewel in his crown because he didn't even come to the Wednesday night prayer services at church. I gave so much more money to missions and I taught Sunday school, and I only have two jewels in my crown! Why is his crown twice the size of mine?"

This whole picture is reminiscent of teenagers measuring who has the latest shoes or the most stylish clothes on the first day of a new school year! No, your salvation was bought and paid for by Jesus Himself. And the past-due note that recorded the debt for your sins was stamped "paid-in-full" when Jesus rose from the dead.

Now that you are a member of God's family, you have worth that is equal to the worth of Jesus' life given in exchange for you. You have a purpose. You are called to use your talents, abilities, and the gifts God entrusted to you for His glory and to build His kingdom.

Write out the next verse in Ephesians 2 (verse 10).

_____

_____

_____

God prepared in advance that you should walk in good works, obeying God and placing His priorities at the top of your to-do list. To do otherwise is…well…why would you do otherwise? Why would you put your own desires ahead of the God who made you and loves you? Why do Christians shrink away from obeying God and place their own plans ahead of His?

Take a look at another familiar passage regarding the Christian new birth.

Write out 2 Corinthians 5:17.

_____

_____

This verse is often quoted and memorized to reinforce the truth that God has created a completely new person in us when we receive Christ. Every old, sinful habit is forgiven when you begin your new life in Christ. And God has done this for a purpose. We can't stop reading there, however!

Write out verses 18 through 20.

_____

_____

_____

_____

You now represent the kingdom of God to the world! Your actions represent God to those who do not know Him. You have been called, chosen, and set apart for God's purposes, as His representative to your world. Before returning to our lesson on Saul, record your thoughts on the lines below.

What, according to these verses, is God's purpose for your life?

_____

_____

Obedience to God's Word has nothing to do with gaining entrance to heaven. Living an obedient Christian life will never gain your heavenly Father's approval. Obedience is the means by which you participate with God, building the kingdom of heaven here on earth and demonstrating your love for Him. Through an obedient life, you release God's power to work in your life and in the lives of people around you. This is the purpose of obedience. The opposite, however, is also true. Outside the boundaries of an obedient Christian life, God is hindered from working in and through you, or in and through the lives of those around you.

Write out Isaiah 59:1-2.

_____

_____

_____

_____

God's kingdom is ruled by love, and as such He will never leave or forsake you. Whenever you call to Him, He listens and responds. But any sin, outwardly deliberate or done in secret, will separate you from God's presence, power, and purpose in your life. Disobedience creates a barrier that prevents God from being able to answer your prayers. He waits for you to come to Him, to empty your hands of your own plans and desires, and say, _Here I am, send me! I come to do Your will, O God._

With these thoughts in mind, let's return to our study of Saul. Saul had an obedience problem. His internal motivations were based on other desires than glorifying the God who made him king.

Look back at 1 Samuel 15:24-25. What was Saul saying was more important to him than obeying God's personal request?

_____

_____

The event we have been considering this week was the final straw in a long pattern of self-seeking decisions which spanned Saul's entire reign. God does not follow a "one-strike-and-you're-out" policy. In next week's lesson, we will look more closely at how God had ministered to Saul for over a decade and a half. These events in 1 Samuel 15 were the final sins that cost Saul his kingdom. His life proved the proverb written close to a century later by King Solomon: *A man who remains stiff-necked after many rebukes will suddenly be destroyed — without remedy* (Proverbs 29:1).

How can we learn from Saul and avoid his mistakes? Obedience can be boiled down to three basic principles, each of which must be in place in order for obedience to be true and from the heart.
1. Fearing God
2. Knowing God's Word
3. Maintaining a pure heart

Let's examine each of these three principles. We will look at the first two today, and the third tomorrow.

1. Fearing God

The phrase "fearing God" sounds archaic, doesn't it? We know that our God is a God of love, so what is there to fear? Our God is a God of love, but He is also a God of justice, righteousness, magnificent power, and, thankfully, wonderful kindness and long-lasting patience. The concept of fearing God recognizes that He made everything, and you owe everything in your life to Him.

Job is a perfect example of a man who learned to truly fear God. Job endured suffering for no apparent reason, all the while insisting to his friends that he had done nothing wrong to deserve what had happened to him. The book of Job takes over twenty chapters for Job to insist to his three obtuse friends that his sin had not brought these difficulties into his life. He was blameless, and in exasperation, he looked to heaven and finally demanded, "God, show Yourself and answer me! I have called, and yet You have hidden Your face from me. Why is this happening to me?" (See Job 23.)

God appeared, but He didn't answer Job's question. God's response followed more along the lines of how a father would respond to a teenage son who was arguing about his curfew. The Lord spoke to Job out of a whirlwind and said, "Who are you to question Me? Were you there when I made the heavens? Have you taught the fish to swim or the birds to fly?" (See Job 38-41.)

After measuring his existence against God's majesty, Job learned the lesson of his affliction. In the final chapter, Job fell to the ground and declared:

> *"I know that you can do all things; no plan of yours can be thwarted. You asked, 'Who is this that obscures my counsel without knowledge?' Surely I spoke of things I did not understand, things too wonderful for me to know. You said, 'Listen now, and I will speak; I will question you, and you shall answer me.' My ears had heard of you but now my eyes have seen you. Therefore I despise myself and repent in dust and ashes."*
>
> —Job 42:2-6

Job finally understood his life in perspective to God's majestic power. He had been formed from the dust of the earth by a mighty and loving God. He saw his life in comparison to God, and the Creator of the universe was immeasurable when likened to Job's life. Job was humbled to be in the presence of God, and that humility brought a change in how he viewed his own importance.

Taking on this perspective is the heart of fearing God. When you truly "get" the majesty, power, and scope of God's greatness, your life takes on the position of a servant to a benevolent king. Jesus Himself came to serve and to teach us that through humility and fearing the One who made us, we find power to live the humble, obedient life of a servant.

Read the following verses. Based on what you have learned from the lives of Saul and Job, write your own definition of what it means to "fear God."

Deuteronomy 10:12   Psalm 36:1-4

Matthew 10:28   2 Corinthians 7:1

_____

_____

_____

_____

2. Knowing God's Word

In addition to fearing God, knowing His Word can give your life specific direction and allow you to be obedient to Him. Proverbs 16:6 says that he who fears God will depart from evil. When you have fully experienced God's greatness, love, and the majesty of His power, you can look to heaven and say, "Your will, Lord, not mine."

The primary way you come to know God's will is through His Word. Attending church services once a week only begins the process of hearing and understanding God's Word. Without personal study of the Bible, you will never understand the great plans God has for you, and you will quickly run out of energy to pursue God's plans and heart. You may even be led down blind alleys that appear to be God's will, but inevitably will cause you to depart from God's plan for your life.

Psalm 119 is the longest chapter of the Bible, but every stanza and verse describe the blessings of a deep understanding of God's Word. Here are a few of the verses in this psalm:

> *Blessed are they who keep his statutes and seek him with all their heart.*
>
> —Verse 2

> *I seek you with all my heart; do not let me stray from your commands. I have hidden your word in my heart that I might not sin against you.*
>
> —Verses 10-11

> *Your statutes are my delight; they are my counselors.*
>
> —Verse 24

If your law had not been my delight, I would have perished in my affliction.

—Verse 92

In the New Testament, Jesus placed the same importance on knowing and obeying God's Word when He told His followers this:

"I am the vine; you are the branches. If a man remains in me and I in him, he will bear much fruit; apart from me you can do nothing. If anyone does not remain in me, he is like a branch that is thrown away and withers; such branches are picked up, thrown into the fire and burned. If you remain in me and my words remain in you, ask whatever you wish, and it will be given you. This is to my Father's glory, that you bear much fruit, showing yourselves to be my disciples."

—John 15:5-8

It is not possible to separate a fruitful life — one that hears and follows God's will wholeheartedly — from a life that remains deeply attached to reading and following God's Word.

As a final exercise for today, read through Psalm 119. On the lines below, write ten blessings promised in this passage to someone who reads, studies, and makes God's Word a part of their everyday life.

_____

_____

_____

_____

_____

_____

_____

_____

_____

_____

Day Five: Following God with a Pure Heart

Saul completely missed the point of God's request for him — primarily because he did not have a pure heart before God. Saul was asked to obliterate the Amalekite army. God had His reasons, and Saul was to be the divine implement to carry out those designs. However, the pressure from his troops and their desires affected his decision. Maybe his own squeamishness regarding the severity of the Lord's directive, or his own selfishness led him to question if it was really that important for him to kill everything. But God's simple and straightforward instructions were to kill *everything*.

The tension between these two polar forces — God's will which points in one direction and your own desires pulling in the other — defines the most important aspect of a changed life. When the heat is on, and you do not understand the ins and outs of what you are called to do, will you obey God, or will you take a step back and look for an easier, more reasonable path? Will you follow God with all your heart, and trust Him with the consequences of what you can't see or don't understand? This was the test that Saul repeatedly failed, and it was the ultimate reason that God "repented that He had made Saul king over Israel."

There is nothing worse than being caught in the middle of a difficult decision. On the one hand is what you know is right, the best choice, and on the other hand there are personal rewards you may not receive if you make the right choice. But sometimes it boils down to simply trusting that God will work out the details that you can't see. Sometimes, as in Saul's case, making the right choice comes down to simply obeying God and putting His will ahead of your own — no matter what.

Think back to David's life. If there was a consistent theme during the years he lived in the wilderness, it was that David put what he knew to be God's will ahead of his own desires. Some of the men who were with him may have looked at David's actions and said that he was a fool. He could have taken Saul's life many times and ended his desert exile. After all, Samuel had anointed him the king. But David knew it would have contradicted God's will to take the life of another man whom God had anointed. The social norm of the day was not the standard by which David lived. He chose to obey God, even though it meant prolonged suffering for him. But the events changed him because his choices pleased God, and he became a man after God's own heart.

Joseph also chose to remain faithful to his integrity even though his situation was the result of his brothers' injustice against him. As a slave, in Potiphar's house, and in jail, Joseph continually passed the tests that Saul failed. When the pressure was on, and everything around him supported a decision to become bitter and hateful, he didn't. By allowing the grace of God to work in his life, Joseph rose to a place of influence not only because he was selected for the job, but also because he allowed God to work in his life and prepare him for the task to which he had been called.

Saul, however, chose the miserable existence somewhere between wholehearted submission to God's will and the pursuit of his own desires. He didn't enjoy the blessings of God because he did not fully submit to God. But he couldn't enjoy the pleasure of sin, because he knew that what he was doing was wrong. He was in a wretched place, and the tension between his carnal desires and selfishness and his hopes for a godly life finally tore the kingdom from his hands.

Below are listed some of the verses containing blessings promised for you when you surrender your whole heart to God. But there are also warnings given regarding a life that tries to live in the "no-man's-land" that lies somewhere between surrender and selfishness.

Read each of these passages and summarize them on the lines provided.
Jeremiah 29:11-13

_____

_____

_____

_____

Psalm 34:10

_____

_____

_____

_____

Psalm 86:12

_____

_____

_____

_____

Jeremiah 24:7

_____

_____

_____

_____

Joshua 24:14-15

_____

_____

_____

_____

Matthew 22:37-40

_____

_____

_____

_____

Our God is a consistent God. The Old Testament has been fulfilled by the New. The Old Testament law has been fulfilled in Jesus Christ, and we have a new covenant of salvation by faith. Yet throughout the entirety of Scripture, those factors which are crucial to a relationship with God remain the same. Serving Him with a unified, whole heart is one of the key elements of a faith that will ultimately transform your heart.

As this week's lesson draws to a close, there are just two more questions to answer. The first is, what or whom do you really love? This question does not refer to your spouse, kids, or family. If Jesus walked into the room where you are sitting right now and asked you this question, how would you answer? Is He at the top of your list? Have you given God the right to everything in your life? Have you given Him permission to poke into any locked closet, or are there things you are holding back?

Write your thoughts on the lines below.

_____

_____

_____

_____

The final question is a follow-up question to the answer you just gave. Regardless of how much devotion you give God today, what kind of life do you want to live in the long run? If you want to live a partially devoted life, be honest about that! If there are specific areas in which you want Christ to rule as Lord, but you don't know how to let go of your own concerns in those areas, write that in the form of a prayer below. Whatever your level of surrender to Jesus is, write it out. Conclude by telling Him what you really desire in your love relationship with Him. He is waiting to hear in your own words.

Record your thoughts in the lines below.

_____

_____

_____

_____

_____

_____

Father God,

My life has followed a path that at times seems completely surrendered to Your will and Your purpose. But then there are times that I would rather forget, when my own selfish desires cloud my vision and consume the divine life You placed in my heart. Lord, I want to be like David and Joseph. I want to look at my life and see that You are present in every desire of my heart, that You are there in every minute of every hour. Father, take my life and let it be ever, only, all for Thee. Amen.

Week Nine: Summary

But what things were gain to me, those I counted loss for Christ. Yea doubtless, and I count all things but loss for the excellency of the knowledge of Christ Jesus my Lord: for whom I have suffered the loss of all things, and do count them but dung, that I may win Christ, And be found in him, not having mine own righteousness, which is of the law, but that which is through the faith of Christ, the righteousness which is of God by faith: That I may know him, and the power of his resurrection, and the fellowship of his sufferings, being made conformable unto his death; If by any means I might attain unto the resurrection of the dead. Not as though I had already attained, either were already perfect: but I follow after, if that I may apprehend that for which also I am apprehended of Christ Jesus. Brethren, I count not myself to have apprehended: but this one thing I do, forgetting those things which are behind, and reaching forth unto those things which are before, I press toward the mark for the prize of the high calling of God in Christ Jesus.

—Philippians 3:7-14 KJV

This week's lessons have introduced you to some new ideas about Saul and the ways in which God wanted to work in his life. What is one new idea that you have learned this week? If there is one thought or idea that God used to grab your attention, write it on the lines below.

_____

_____

_____

_____

_____

_____

_____

Saul

A Divided Heart's Slow Descent into Compromise

You are always moving in the direction of your most dominant thoughts.

—Brian Tracy

Day One: Take a Look at God's Word

Saul's encounter with King Agag and the Amalekites is the climactic conclusion of the first period of King Saul's reign. This failure marked a crossroads in his life. After this campaign, Saul's anointing passed to David, and over the coming years, Saul slowly began to realize that David would replace him on Israel's throne. At that point, David's life catapulted onto the biblical stage, and God began to move in his life to train him to be Israel's new king.

The events from David's life in the first section of this workbook occurred after the events we considered in last week's study. This week's lessons take one further step backward in time to the first years of Saul's reign. From the time of his inauguration until the fateful battle with the Amalekites, Saul reigned a decade and a half. He was Israel's first appointed king, taking the throne after the Israelites' demand to have a king like the nations around them. They had felt weak and vulnerable without a central political figure to run the country and lead a standing army.

First Samuel 9 and 10 provide background to our glimpse into the reign of Saul; these chapters describe how Samuel was sent to Saul, anointed him king, and then in a public ceremony presented him to the nation. Unfortunately, Saul's reign did not measure up to the hopes and dreams of Samuel, the people — or of God.

At the end of last week's study, one question remained. What was behind the severe nature of God's response to Saul's disobedience? Was this event with the Amalekites a singularly poor choice of Saul's? If so, why did God react with such finality and remove Saul from leadership? Or was Saul's refusal to obey the final straw in a pattern that had been established over time, and that now prevented Saul from being able to even hear the Lord's commands?

This week's lessons consider three other events that took place during Saul's early reign. While Saul was God's choice for Israel's first king, we will discover that Saul never became the man God desired and Israel needed him to be. His lifestyle illustrated a pattern of divided interests and personal insecurity. The decisions that sprang from these maladies created a maelstrom from which he never escaped. Wrestling with divided interests and insecurities, Saul chose repeatedly to put his own feelings and interests ahead of God's purposes. They clouded his vision, obscuring from his view what could have been wise choices. And it ultimately led to his failure as a king.

For this week, we will look at the events that are recorded in 1 Samuel 9 through 14. In a quiet restful place, read these chapters and reflect on what took place. Then record your thoughts and any insights you glean from each chapter before proceeding to tomorrow's historical perspective.

Chapter 9

_____

_____

_____

_____

_____

Chapter 10

_____

_____

_____

_____

_____

Chapter 11

_____

_____

_____

_____

_____

Chapter 12

_____

_____

_____

_____

_____

Chapter 13

_____

_____

_____

_____

_____

Chapter 14

_____

_____

_____

_____

_____

Day Two: Saul's Brash Response

As a new king, Saul's first challenge came from Nahash, the Ammonite. At that time, the young Israelite nation did not have a standing army; after having lived in the Promised Land for nearly 325 years, they were still little more than a collection of loosely-knit tribes living in small towns scattered across the arid countryside. The Hebrews struggled to establish a singular political and cultural identity in the region. Since Joshua had died, the nation was ruled by a series of judges, and they experienced rotating cycles of peace followed by military incursions by their neighbors.

Read 1 Samuel 11:1-11.
What was the threat the Ammonites made?

_____

_____

What did Saul do when he heard the news?

_____

_____

How did he motivate the people to action?

_____

_____

How was the battle won?

_____

_____

The Ammonites' threat represented just one of many skirmishes between the Israelites and the tribes who lived in the area. The young nation had begun to weary of the constant clashes, and this being Saul's first challenge after being anointed as king, he wanted to make a statement that change was in the air! He wanted to establish himself as Israel's leader, and especially as a formidable opponent to the neighboring combatants. Saul issued a call to arms in a way that is typical of new leaders. He wanted action — and he wanted it immediately! He felt the call to go — a call that had come from the Spirit of God (see verse 6) — and he knew he was to eliminate the Ammonite threat. But he acted rashly on that call, especially in the way he instilled the desire for action in the rest of the nation. In verse 7, we see Saul's brash response. He slaughtered a yoke of oxen in the public market, personally cutting the beasts into pieces, and then he sent these animal carcasses by cart to every corner of the kingdom. The cart drivers carried this message: "Whoever does not join us to defend our nation against the Ammonites, the same will be done to his animals."

There are many ways to call people to action and incite their patriotism to defend their homeland. The problem wasn't that Saul desired to motivate his people — remember, he had been called and anointed by God to lead them and to take action in situations such as this. What is in question was the way Saul responded to the impending threat. He did communicate the need of the moment and his desire to take action. And he certainly did so in a manner that motivated his people — an army soon gathered to prepare for war. But Saul's approach to the situation did not build confidence in his citizens. Saul's example was not one that elicited national pride in the people and respect for their king. Instead, Saul began his reign by choosing fear as a motivator for his people. Rather than responding out of a desire to build up their new kingdom, the soldiers gathered out of fear for their own well-being. Saul did not demonstrate positive leadership over a well-prepared army. Instead, he hit the table with his fist and said, "Do this or else!"

It is said that you can't push a string, and you can't herd cats. But you can motivate people through a number of positive methods. By watching the way someone chooses to inspire others, you can discover much about the person himself. The way a person interacts with others, their family members, or the company for which they work, speaks volumes about what is important to that person. What you hold as valuable, and what has a hold on your heart, will make itself visible in your choices. And in the end, the kind of family, company, or nation you create will be a reflection of your own heart.

From the moment of creation, God's design is that we would give birth to beings like ourselves. Biologically, fish spawn other fish, birds lay eggs that hatch into other birds, and humans give birth to humans. This principle is also demonstrated in terms of our heart and character. Parents with short fuses tend to raise children who also struggle with keeping emotional control. Parents who demonstrate understanding and empathy will often raise children who are open, giving, and compassionate. Within the corporate culture, employees who work for a ruthless CEO, often in order to survive, will begin to demonstrate the same cutthroat, "rise-to-the-top-at-any-cost" mentality. But a company with a captain at the helm who is committed to serving and investing in his community will have the same well-earned reputation.

Compare this principle of human dynamics to Saul's actions. His edict elicited fear. The extreme nature of Saul's conduct demonstrated a lack of security, a lack of confidence in his own leadership. Look back at 1 Samuel 10:1, 6, and 9. These verses record the events that took place on the day Samuel anointed Saul as king. The Spirit of God fell upon Saul, and the text even says that God would turn Saul into a new man. But the arduous process God chose to put David through in preparation for leadership was not present in the events that prepared Saul to lead. And as a result, when Saul was under pressure, his choices sprang from his yet unaltered heart.

Consider the differences between David and Saul. What was different about their rise to leadership, and about the way they later led the kingdom?

_____

_____

_____

_____

How did their earlier personal actions and experiences foreshadow the kings they would later become?

_____

_____

_____

When you are in a situation that requires you to take action, does fear play a role in your decision-making process? Could fear ever successfully lead you to a positive course of action, or does it drive you to "respond now and worry about the consequences later"? In a situation that causes you to be fearful, are you apt to find positive, proactive solutions? Chances are good that fear will elicit a knee-jerk response and inspire foolish decisions. But on the other hand, confidence breeds confidence. Like gives birth to like. Saul brought his own insecurities into his army.

God was gracious to His people, and the results of this first battle were successful. As the Israelites routed the Ammonites, they took their first collective step toward becoming a unified nation. Saul was now affirmed in the position of their king, leader, victor, and champion, but he still had much to learn about leading his country and surrendering himself to God's will.

The decisions you make on the job, in family relationships, or even in how to spend your income, are choices that are influenced by your heart and your desires. If you are led by fear or insecurity, you will make choices that consistently produce disruptive consequences. Unfortunately, the motives behind our decisions are often visible only in life's rearview mirror. Only after the event passes and you are left wondering what happened, can you begin to identify the "why" of a particular decision. Wise decisions tend to produce peaceful and positive results, while unwise choices eventually lead to broken relationships as you place your own personal safety, reputation, or desires ahead of the well-being of others.

At the beginning of each of David and Joseph's "desert experiences," they were not yet ready to lead. They had not yet learned their need for utter dependence on God. They did not have a deep enough relationship with their Maker, nor did they have the character that would allow them to be the men God had called them to be. Their "character" had to catch up with their "calling." Unfortunately, as Saul took the throne, his heart was in the same unprepared condition, but he did not learn to rely on God as his Father, Provider, and Guide, and the demands of his life proved to be too great a weight to carry.

God is continually working in your life to empower you to live for Him today, and equip you to serve Him more fully tomorrow. By allowing Him to weigh your motives and sort out the reasons behind what you do, you can open the door for God to draw you closer to Him. The cost of a deeper relationship with God is allowing Him to purify your selfish motives.

One way to draw closer to God is to leave behind the selfish and sometimes self-destructive traditions onto which you have held.

Write out Ezekiel 11:19-20.

_____

_____

_____

You could read this passage and assume that it refers to what God does in your life when you begin your Christian walk. God begins to change your heart and places His Spirit within you when you receive Christ as your Savior. But while that is true, this scripture was written to God's people — those who already had a relationship with Him. The Israelites were being given an admonition to draw closer to God, so that He could continue to work in their hearts and lives, and in them as a collective community. The process of change begins when you are born again, but it is a work that God continues every day. God wants to be able to say that you are a person who seeks after His heart and lives in tune with His heartbeat.

Consider one of the events you described in your previous weeks' journaling. Hopefully you have discovered that God was at work, even if the days were dark or difficult. You should have also discovered that His desire is to draw you closer to Himself through these events. Now ask yourself these questions: What attitudes in your own life may have contributed to the situation you described? What could you have done that would have been more Christ-like? How might your own motives or desires have helped to cause the difficulty?

Record your thoughts below.

_____

_____

_____

Saul's reign began on a high note, but his motives set the stage for trouble. His selfishness pulled out the rubber stopper at the bottom of the tub, and as the water slowly drained, his poor choices created a swirling vortex from which he could not escape. As the water first began to drain, there was no reason to take notice. His seemingly smaller choices at the beginning of his reign did not appear to be an important issue at that time. But Saul had begun the descending spiral of spiritual ineffectiveness, and his insecurity and self-interest eventually cost him the throne.

Principle Ten: The weaknesses in your character can lie hidden at first, but they will come to light in the decisions that you make. Mixed motives will eventually betray the self-centered nature of your choices and priorities.

How can you see principle ten evidenced in Saul's life?

_____

_____

_____

How can you see it in your own life?

_____

_____

_____

Day Three: Stepping Outside of God's Boundaries

Saul's next military encounter pitched his new army against the Philistines in a skirmish that was the beginning of ongoing conflict between these two regional powers. The Philistines viewed the Israelites as "squatters" who were occupying their homeland. In response to the gathering threat, Saul brought his army together, and they prepared for battle at Gilgal. Just to the north, and within sight of the fledgling Israelite army, the Philistines gathered their huge forces at Michmash. They possessed chariots, charioteers, and an army that far outnumbered Israel's forces.

Saul's forces became so intimidated that they began to sneak away from the battlefield. Some hid in caves, and others sought cover in the rocky hills. Some of Israel's forces even traveled to the west and crossed the Jordan River to escape the ensuing conflict.

Sensing his need for God's blessing, Saul sent word to Samuel. He wanted Samuel to offer sacrifices and pray for the army before they engaged the Philistine hosts. Saul sent his request, but Samuel was delayed much longer than Saul had hoped. As he watched the Philistines' army continue to grow in number, Saul knew he could only hold to the remainder of his troops for a limited time. Soon he would risk losing the battle by default, for a lack of men to fight. The pressure pushed Saul to make yet another rash decision.

Reread 1 Samuel 13:1-15.

What was Saul's poor decision?

_____

_____

_____

What was Samuel's response?

_____

_____

_____

Because of his impatience, Saul offered sacrifices to the Lord himself before they headed into battle. The coals of the altar were still glowing as Samuel arrived and rebuked the king severely.

The severity of this response again may seem out of proportion to the infraction, until we have an understanding of Israel's social structure. In the organization that God established in His nation, the king was actually an afterthought. Saul was placed in the position of political leader only at the request of the people, but God's authority in the nation remained firm: He was in charge. God's social order for the Israelites was that of a theocracy, not a monarchy. The priests were the appointed ones to offer sacrifices and intercede to God for the people. God designed a very specific order and there were no allowances for a political king to operate in a spiritual office. Ministering before the Lord was the priests' work, and by assuming Samuel's mantle, Saul ignored the boundaries God had set for him, and he miserably failed yet another test of how to respond to pressure. And this time his offense took him far outside the boundaries of God's law.

Why was God so angry with Saul? After all, the needs of His people were pressing. His troops were anxious, and the king knew that his greatest asset in this military campaign was positive morale. Saul risked losing not only more soldiers, but the mental edge necessary for his army to wage war. But God chose to wait and in so doing, to test this man whom He had called to lead His people. Would Saul trust only what he could see, or would he trust God's provision?

Saul's response was disappointing, and his efforts to maintain the cohesiveness of his army also failed. Saul was left with just 600 men. His attempt to gain God's favor had backfired, and the battle that could have finished off the Philistines was not to be. The Philistines continued to be a menace, launching campaign after campaign and causing an ongoing tribulation for the Israelite nation. The Philistines threatened Israel throughout Saul's rule and into David's reign before God finally brought rest to His people from this oppressor.

The result of his displaced priorities caused fear to hang like a curtain between Saul and his God — a silent, deafening curtain. Saul never learned that the battle remains in God's hands, and he voided out the process that was successful in David and Joseph's lives — the process that forged within them the character of God. And that leads us to our next principle:

Principle Eleven: Tension, struggle, and conflict will always be a part of life. Our faith rises to new heights by overcoming these challenges.

In your life, there are rarely times when a single decision will bring such devastating consequences. But one decision will lead to another, and soon a pattern begins to emerge. In the everyday decisions of life, your trust in God becomes most evident. Will you look to your own efforts as the source of your confidence? Does your life consist of monuments you have raised to celebrate your own efforts or to glorify God for His blessing and provision? The most important question is not how much money you make or the kind of lifestyle you are able to create for yourself. The real question is, who is in charge of your life, and to whom do you give glory? Whom do you trust when the chips are down? Or whom do you praise when events are going well?

God's desire is that you will look to Him and be desperate for Him in all circumstances, at all times, and in all things. Psalm 40 puts it this way:

> *I waited patiently for the LORD; and he inclined unto me, and heard my cry. He brought me up also out of an horrible pit, out of the miry clay, and set my feet upon a rock, and established my goings. And he hath put a new song in my mouth, even praise unto our God: many shall see it, and fear, and shall trust in the LORD. Blessed is that man that maketh the LORD his trust, and respecteth not the proud, nor such as turn aside to lies. Many, O LORD my God, are thy wonderful works which thou hast done, and thy thoughts which are to us-ward: they cannot be reckoned up in order unto thee: if I would declare and speak of them, they are more than can be numbered. Sacrifice and offering thou didst not desire; mine ears hast thou opened: burnt-offering and sin-offering hast thou not required. Then said I, Lo, I come: in the volume of the book it is written of me, I delight to do thy will, O my God: yea, thy law is within my heart.*
>
> —Verses 1-8 KJV

How do these verses speak to Saul's sin in our lesson today?

_____

_____

_____

What does God desire more than sacrifices and offerings?

_____

_____

_____

Read the following scripture passages and then in the lines below, write a prayer to the Lord, recommitting yourself to obedience to His Word and His plan and purpose for your life.

Psalm 42:1-8

Psalm 139

Isaiah 40:25-31

_____

_____

_____

_____

_____

_____

_____

_____

_____

Day Four: Sitting under a Pomegranate Tree

Saul's divided heart rested on a foundation of self-doubt. And his actions sowed further seeds of doubts that rippled into ever-widening circles. He did not learn to stop, take an inventory of what he was doing, make a change, and trust God for provision and guidance. As he continued to repeat previous mistakes, Saul's doubts and fears spread from his own life into the lives of those whom he led.

Someone once said that you can't tell a pitcher's contents until it is jostled and some of the liquid spills out. Through life's jostling process, God allows you to see what's hidden in the pitcher of your own heart. Your goal becomes to allow God to change those contents, to build godly character in you to make you into His image. But God will never force you into making that choice. It is up to you whether you will learn to draw near to God and allow Him to change you, or you will continue to repeat the same mistakes.

As Saul's war with the Philistines continued, it becomes clear to us that Saul did not understand why his efforts were so ineffective. His first skirmishes with other foes were mighty victories, but he was suddenly in a difficult position. In 1 Samuel 14, a bewildered Saul sat under a pomegranate tree wondering what to do next. His lieutenants, generals, and troops waited nearby. Samuel had not been seen for days, possibly months. Saul's indecision was eating away at the company's confidence like leprosy. He was angry with himself over the ongoing war and could not understand why the conflict was dragging on. The Philistines had raided Israel's supply lines in three separate and successful campaigns. They had kidnapped many of the blacksmiths and had taken much of their military hardware, leaving the Israelites weaponless and without the ability to mount an armed attack.

Read 1 Samuel 14:1-46.

By this time, Saul's son Jonathan was becoming a leader in his own right. At the outset of this conflict, he was sent on a scouting mission that separated him from his father's command post. Jonathan hungered to bring his father victory, and with his armor bearer, he crept quietly into the cleft between two large rocks. From their vantage point they spotted a Philistine garrison across the valley on the opposite ridge. At that moment, Jonathan spoke words that could have taught his father much about trusting God.

Write out Jonathan's words to his armor bearer (found in verse 6).

_____

_____

_____

Jonathan did not look at his situation and say to himself, *We're outnumbered — this is a bad idea. Let's head back to camp and get reinforcements.* His confidence did not rest in himself, but in his God.

Jonathan and his armor bearer pressed forward, and with God's blessing, put the entire Philistine garrison to retreat. Jonathan's faith-filled actions turned the tide of the war. When the Israelites who were still hiding in the surrounding countryside heard the rising tumult of victory, they came out of the caves and joined the fray. The skirmish created such a disturbance that its noise finally reached Saul's pomegranate tree. By the time Saul got up and arrived on the scene, the Philistines were in complete disarray, and Saul was able to order an advance.

However, once again his fears surfaced and his rash decision-making nearly caused a disaster.

Write out Saul's rash decree (found in verse 24).

_____

_____

_____

How was this decree another reflection of the extremism that we have already seen in Saul's life?

_____

_____

_____

Jonathan was at the head of the advancing Israelite army. Although he was responsible for the campaign, he was not aware of his father's edict. Once the army joined Jonathan, the Philistines were pushed back into the mountains a distance of five to seven miles, and from there, the campaign advanced on foot through the hills and woods. Israel's tactics, brought about by God's direct leadership over Jonathan, rendered the Philistines' chariots useless! But during the final miles of the campaign, the men were falling victim to exhaustion rather than the Philistines.

Unfortunately, Saul's extreme decision prohibited anyone from eating until they had finished the job. Because Jonathan didn't know of his father's decree, when he grew weak, he stopped and scooped some honeycomb from a nearby beehive. As he enjoyed a needed break, resting and eating the honey, his strength was recharged. But when the others caught up to him, they were shocked and immediately asked, "What are you doing?!"

Jonathan responded like most young men would have in a similar situation: "I was hungry! We've made great progress in the battle, and I needed to regain my strength." When they told Jonathan of King Saul's command, his response was telling. It shows that Jonathan had likely been a victim of his father's extremism before, because it was far out of character for a son who is fighting for his father's kingdom.

What was Jonathan's response (found in verses 29-30)?

_____

_____

_____

In effect, Jonathan was saying, "I don't believe that it's God's desire for His people to be placed under such extreme demands — especially when it causes them to lose their focus and their ability to serve Him. My father should understand this!"

A godly influencer and a true leader is aware of and respects the needs of those around him. His actions are a reflection of the care and compassion that God has for the people he is leading. A godly person has allowed God to change their heart. God's cares become their own, and they lead with that ever on their minds. But Saul's vision was blurred to his troops' needs because of his own struggles and insecurities.

A similar event in David's life demonstrates how a leader after God's own heart would have handled such a situation.

Read 1 Chronicles 11:13-19.

David and his troops were in the middle of a military campaign. They had been in the field for months, their supplies were low, and David was thirsty. His mightiest men saw their leader's fatigue, and out of love for a king who would lay down his own life for them, they chose to risk their own lives to meet his needs. There was water behind the Philistines' battle lines. So that evening, David's commanders broke through the lines and filled a water skin for their king. When they returned to David, he realized that these men had risked their lives to present him with their gift. And David's response was to pour the water on the ground!

In essence, David was saying, *"No!* I will not drink this water even though I am thirsty. I will not enjoy the fruit of actions that put your lives at risk!" David was saying, "You have taken on my job — that's my calling. I'm the one responsible to provide water for us. *I'm* the one who should take this kind of risk to provide for *your* needs!"

I doubt that David's lieutenants were angry at his decision. I doubt that their pride was hurt at his refusal to accept their gift. They learned from a man who led by example, not by edict. And as morning broke the next day, I am confident that each of these men desired more deeply to give their lives for David. What a difference between David's leadership and Saul's before him!

The apostle John tells us that perfect love casts out all fear (see 1 John 4:18). David and Joseph both learned this truth through the trials of darkness and despair. Sometimes it takes coming to the end of our own abilities before we completely surrender to our loving Father and let Him into all aspects of our lives. God will often use a furnace to melt the impurities of fear and self-protectionism from our lives so that we are free to serve Him without reservation.

How does your life reflect godly leadership, such as what David displayed?

_____

_____

_____

_____

_____

In what ways may you act like Saul at times? How could you change those patterns of behavior?

_____

_____

_____

_____

_____

_____

_____

_____

Day Five: Is Saul in Your Mirror?

Because we are complex and complicated human beings, our motives are rarely simple or black and white. Our motives behind a particular choice can be based on a number of different priorities. But when Jesus said that our highest calling should be to "love the Lord your God with all your heart, mind, soul, and strength, and your neighbor as yourself" (see Luke 10:27), He defined a course of action that requires surrendering to His leadership in every area of our lives. There is no room for compromise with the word all!

Some Christians try to "water down" Jesus' teaching in this area — maybe not explicitly in the words that they say, but their thoughts and actions belie their heart attitudes. They are inwardly hoping to find a way of smoothing the edges of Jesus' words: *Surely God doesn't expect me to give my whole life to Him?! That might make me some kind of religious extremist!* Many Christians have so compartmentalized their lives that God only "fits" into certain time slots, and their level of commitment does not extend beyond their spiritual "to-do" list:

• Go to church on Sunday mornings
• Attend Tuesday night Bible studies — if nothing else conflicts in the schedule
• Go to Wednesday night services — if they're not too tired
• Make sure the kids are involved in the youth group
• Try to put some money in the offering plate each week

But the nagging question remains: *Am I loving Him with my whole heart?* The key to truly answering this question lies in discerning the difference between *activity* and a *heart attitude.* What we really treasure will be the pivot around which our lives revolve.

Have you given God ownership of every area of your life? If you had to make a choice tomorrow that honored God, but cost you your career, what would you do? If you were asked by a close friend to accompany her to an abortion that resulted from a secret affair, would you help her still the life of the child in her womb? Or would you counsel her to save the child, regardless of what it meant for your relationship? If God has called you to be a doctor, or if He's called you to missions in a third-world country, obey Him. If God has allowed you to live in a quarter-million-dollar house or a one-bedroom apartment, your home can be a place where Christ is King.

Heart issues are rarely simple. They tear at what you hold as important, but when God challenges all that you know and what you are willing to do, you can be sure that His desire is for you to surrender more of your heart to Him, so that He can bless your life with more of Himself.

When God acts through circumstances, He often chooses difficulty or painful situations to loosen the steely grasp you hold on things you call your own. God used situations in Joseph and David's lives to effect changes in their priorities. But the Creator of the universe is also moving in your life to reveal more of Himself to you.

The final questions in today's lesson can be some of the most difficult to answer. No one wants to look in the mirror and say, "Yep, I blew it!" When situations swirl out of our control, admitting responsibility in setting them into motion can be extremely difficult. Jesus called this kind of admission *repentance*. He calls you to forsake your own selfish life in order to embrace His life.

As you have considered the life of Saul these past two weeks, have you seen him in the mirror staring back at you? We have all made similar mistakes as Saul did at one point or another in our lives. But what made Saul's situation such a disaster was that *he never repented or changed his ways*. His heart attitude never changed, and he lost everything that God had planned for him.

Reflect on what you've learned so far from the lives of David, Joseph, and Saul. Take the time to reread the primary thoughts and ideas you have recorded at the end of each chapter until this point, and then prayerfully consider your answers to the next few questions.

In what ways has the pattern of your life followed that of David or Joseph?

_____

_____

_____

_____

_____

Has there ever been a time when God's blessings departed from what you were doing as it did in Saul's life? If so, describe the situation.

_____

_____

_____

What was your responsibility in the way things turned out?

_____

_____

_____

What was the outcome of your actions?

_____

_____

_____

Since the time of that situation, have you recovered and learned how to follow God in the decisions that you make?

_____

_____

_____

_____

Someone once defined the word foolishness as making the same decision over and over, but expecting different results each time. Are you repeating the same poor choices over and over? If so, what can you do to break this pattern?

In what specific ways have you learned to allow God's heart to influence what you want and what you are seeking?

In some cases your decisions may have created ongoing situations that are still swirling. You may feel as if someone pulled the stopper in your bathtub, and you are caught in the swirling eddy as it slips down the drain. You may be like Saul, sitting under the pomegranate tree, wondering how you got into the trouble you're in — and how in the world you will get out. The Philistines are amassing, and you don't have a clue about what to do.

If this describes you, I would ask you to find a friend or a mentor, someone who can encourage you and provide you with wise counsel. In our self-sufficient culture, admitting that you can benefit from the advice of others is often difficult to do. The greatest obstacle to making changes in your life may be admitting that things aren't perfect. However, if God has taught you valuable lessons about His love for you through this study, He is already drawing you to Himself to change your heart. He may also want to provide a brother, sister, mentor, or friend to walk beside you in this process.

As you finish this week's lessons, take time to pray, and bring the needs in your life to your Father. Let Him into every area of your heart and your life, and ask Him to bring into your life the people you need to support you as you grow.

Father,

There comes a time when I have done everything I can do, and I am still unable to keep the promises I have made or make the choices that I know would please You. Father, I have learned that David was surrounded by a band of close friends who gave him strength, and Saul tried to lead while remaining alone under a pomegranate tree. Father, there are times when I see Saul's face in my mirror. I see selfish decisions. I see failed attempts to do good. Father, I ask You to bring into my life the people and resources I need to grow to become more like You. I give You all of my heart, and ask You to create a clean heart in me, and renew in me a right spirit. Amen.

Week Ten: Summary

A friend loveth at all times, and a brother is born for adversity.

—Proverbs 17:17 KJV

Iron sharpeneth iron; so a man sharpeneth the countenance of his friend.

—Proverbs 27:17 KJV

This lesson has completed our study of Saul, and the ways in which God wanted to work in his life. If there is one insight or idea that summarizes what you have learned so far, write it on the lines below.

_____

_____

_____

_____

_____

_____

_____

_____

_____

Now we will turn to our final character study — that of King Hezekiah, who ruled in the divided kingdom, many years after the reigns of Saul and David. Hezekiah's rule began on a positive note but ended in disappointment as his heart became divided between serving God and his own self-interest.

Hezekiah

Nursing Divided Interests

For the eyes of the LORD move to and fro throughout the earth that He may strongly support those whose heart is completely His.

—2 Chronicles 16:9 NASB

Day One: Take a Look at God's Word

Three hundred years after King David slept with his fathers, God kept His promises to David's descendants, and his grandsons still occupied Israel's throne. After Solomon's reign, the kingdom was split, divided between Israel to the north and Judah to the south. Throughout this turbulent period in Israel's history, scribes were assigned to record events during each king's reign. These scribes are credited for compiling the books of 2 Samuel, 1 and 2 Kings, and 1 and 2 Chronicles. As each king came to the throne, the first few lines written to describe their reign contained a synopsis which measured them by the benchmark of King David before them. With few exceptions, the first few sentences devoted to the king contained four important pieces of information:

1. Their immediate father's identity;

2. The age at which the king took the throne;

3. The length of his reign; and

4. A line similar to this: "The king served the Lord with all of his heart, like David," or, "The king did not serve the Lord with all his heart, like David his father had."

If you read through the legacies from Solomon's feuding sons all the way to King Hezekiah, you will find that Hezekiah is one of a select few who served the Lord with all his heart near the end of the Israelite nation.

King Hezekiah's legacy is recorded in a number of Old Testament books, and the passages you will read today provide an overview of his reign, describe some important events in his lifetime, and introduce those biblical characters who influenced his life, so that you can gain an understanding of his character and heart.

Write out 2 Kings 18:3.

_____

_____

_____

_____

_____

Hezekiah began his twenty-nine year reign by serving the Lord with all his heart. However, by the end of King Hezekiah's reign, a subtle shift in his priorities was to alter this king's legacy and his country's destiny forever.

As you read the biblical record, even though he seemed to start out well, you will not find King Hezekiah remembered among the greats. Second Kings 18 through 20 records the basic historical record of his reign.

Read 2 Kings 18-20. Imagine yourself as Hezekiah. What would it be like to lead Israel at this time in the nation's turbulent history?

_____

_____

_____

_____

Write your thoughts regarding each chapter below.

2 Kings 18

_____

_____

2 Kings 19

_____

_____

2 Kings 20

_____

_____

Hezekiah lived during the time of another Old Testament writer. The prophet Isaiah was Hezekiah's personal counsel, much in the same way that Samuel guided Saul, and Nathan admonished David. Isaiah preached to all of Israel. Before the northern tribes were conquered by the Babylonians, Isaiah warned them to soften their hearts and return to serving the living God. After the northern kingdom of Israel fell, he turned his attention to the three remaining tribes living in the southern half of the land. He promised that they too would be taken captive like their brothers if they did not forsake their idols and return to worshiping Jehovah alone.

Isaiah had a cameo role in the life of Hezekiah.

What occurred in 2 Kings 20, and how was Isaiah involved?

_____

_____

_____

What was Isaiah's prediction in verses 16-18?

_____

_____

_____

What was Hezekiah's response?

_____

_____

_____

Read 2 Chronicles 32:24-26.

Why was God's judgment to fall on Judah?

_____

_____

_____

What caused judgment to be deferred — for a time?

_____

_____

_____

God had mercy on Hezekiah, despite the divided nature of his heart. As we dig deeper into his life in the final weeks of our study, pray that God would reveal to you the divided areas of your own heart. And ask that He would give you the strength you need to serve Him as David did — with your whole heart.

Day Two: In the Shadow of the Throne

My name is Jochanah. I'm a servant in the house of the kings of Israel in the kingdom of Judah. My father was a servant, as was my grandfather. We are descendants of Mephibosheth, Saul's only remaining offspring to survive after David ascended to the throne. We've lived in the palace for seven generations. Mephibosheth, our ancestor, ate at David's table as David fulfilled his promise to Saul and Jonathan, and our family has been well cared for. We have not known want of any sort while in the king's house these 350 years.

Three kings ago, Josiah offered my family a new start. He gave us a choice: He promised us either a home and a plot of land for our own families, or we could remain in the palace as special servants to the king himself. My great-grandfather's brother accepted the king's gracious offer. He received a small house and planted a vineyard in the fertile hills just south of Jerusalem. His family now lives on a farm a few miles outside of Bethlehem. However, my great-grandfather chose to stay in the king's house. We have never been mistreated, and the favor of David's promise to our ancestor has continued to bless our lives to this day.

Today I serve King Hezekiah. Since my grandfather first taught me about our palace duties, I've watched the kings ascend the throne and then be laid to rest with their fathers. I carried the washbasin for Hezekiah's father, and as a child I would often hide in the shadows of the royal hall as they discussed the day's events. Skirmishes with the Philistines, blessings of God, the prophet's warnings, and prayer for rain…from my corner in the shadows, just behind the door to the king's armory, I listened as men of God led our nation. When Hezekiah took the throne, I was sixteen years old, and I remember well the early days of his kingdom.

Hezekiah's first decree was to eliminate the high places and pull down the altars to Baal. He personally oversaw this work which Josiah, his great-grandfather, had begun. He charged his first in command to remove Baal's priests from their palace home and rid the kingdom of their sins. As a result, God blessed the kingdom. Jehovah's favor returned, and although the splendor of David and Solomon would remain elusive, Hezekiah's devotion to Jehovah brought feelings of hope and greatness to our small kingdom once again. Twenty years have passed since Hezekiah took the throne. During my service I watched many men come and go from his chamber. His political insight won the respect of the neighboring tribes, and the Assyrians and the Babylonians often sent ambassadors to have an audience with him.

Another man who had the king's confidence was Isaiah, the prophet. A frequent visitor to Hezekiah's inner chamber, this small-statured, eccentric man often appeared at times of unique need in the king's life. Isaiah's fiery eyes demanded the attention of those whom he approached. He was slightly bent over as he walked, but the anointing of Jehovah marked every step. Each year on the high days, Isaiah was seated at Hezekiah's right hand. He preached about our brothers to the north, rambling about how their idolatry would bring God's judgment. Most of us thought these were just the musings of an unconventional old man. But fourteen years into Hezekiah's reign, he and Isaiah watched as the Babylonians overran our northern brothers and carried them away as captives. The two men spent much time in the temple during those years. They prayed and worshiped together, asking God to protect our nation.

The inevitable attack came. Sennacherib and the Assyrian army besieged Jerusalem. They mocked our God from outside the walls. They told us not to trust Jehovah, for no gods had saved the other nations they'd overrun. But we knew we served the God who is the Lord of lords. As Isaiah prayed with Hezekiah in the temple, the Lord led the Assyrian army back to their homeland, and then God Himself struck them down in the darkness. The celebrations as a result of that victory were greater than I have seen before or since.

God once again honored our kingdom as we honored Him, and Jehovah's divine supply returned. In the year Sennacherib surrounded the city, we had no opportunity to plant our fields, but we ate what grew on its own as a sign of God's blessing. The next year, as the men worked to repair their homes, we again feasted on crops that grew on their own. The Assyrian army had destroyed our fields, broken our wells, and cut our cisterns into pieces. It was not until the third year that we could plant crops and harvest our fields. But when we honored and trusted God, He brought the protection, provision, and miracles we needed. I yearn for the harvests, celebrations, and the festivals of those days. It has been many years.

At the height of Hezekiah's accomplishments, he was stricken ill. Isaiah appeared in the halls once again, and this time his presence brought solemnity to the palace. He told Hezekiah to put his house in order; it was time for his reign to end. He was going to die.

But why? the king wondered in anguish. *Why, at the height of my success, would God take this from me? Why can't I continue to enjoy the promise of prosperity? Why would God call me home now?*

I stood in my favorite shadow, the same place I had stood as a boy, that day as Hezekiah and Isaiah argued in the palace. Hezekiah coughed and wheezed as his health faltered. Only a miracle from God would heal him, and Hezekiah had seen many miracles. But God had sent Isaiah to say that he was finished. His time on earth was over.

That evening, as Isaiah left, the king fell on the floor beside his bed. He knew the stories of the sacred scrolls, how God had commanded Abraham to sacrifice his son, and that He had halted His hand when He saw Abraham's faithfulness. Hezekiah read the miracles recorded in the pages — how time and time again God relented from His judgment. Hezekiah recounted these events to God as he wept by his bed and once again prayed for healing.

The next day Isaiah returned with instructions on how the king's sickness would be healed. While a wave of joy swept through the palace, Isaiah did not share our jubilation. As he passed me in the hall, I sensed sadness that I had never before encountered. The fire in his eyes that I had come to know so well still burned, but his face carried a weight of disappointment. He had just announced a miracle, a mighty testimony to our God. So why was he stooped, almost shuffling, as he walked? What did he know that we didn't?

When Hezekiah's health returned, we planned celebrations with the neighboring kings once again. Their nobles came to see the king who had been sick unto death and yet recovered. Throughout the festivities, Isaiah stood on the sidelines, distant from his usual place at the king's side. As I brought bowls of fruit and wine to the king, I saw the same look in Isaiah's eyes. His face betrayed the tears that cut a path down through his beard. How could he be so sad in the middle of a celebration? How could this man of God be so somber when God had heard our prayers and healed our king? What did he know?

Hezekiah ruled for fifteen more years. In the third year after his recovery, his son Manasseh was born. When Hezekiah died, Manasseh reigned in his place, taking the throne at the age of twelve. Though he was seen less frequently during Hezekiah's last years, after Manasseh began to rule, Isaiah was never again invited to the king's house. Manasseh was not a man who concerned himself with Jehovah's desires. He rebuilt the high places and filled the land with the idols that his father had torn down. He renewed the sacrifices and defiled the land with innocent blood as he sacrificed children to the gods of our neighbors as Hezekiah's father had done. Manasseh's advisors vainly advised the king that these were the very habits responsible for our northern brothers' judgment. But Manasseh's arrogance would not allow him to listen.

Manasseh's sin exceeded any of the kings' sins I had seen in my lifetime. Under every green tree I watched the people build idols and graven images to the foreign gods, and soon the fate of our northern brothers was our own. Babylon attacked our kingdom. They had already conquered the Assyrians, and we were next. It wouldn't take long for Jerusalem to fall. There was no prayer to Jehovah. There was no hope in the streets. And Isaiah's words were now words of certain judgment. Two days ago, the Babylonian troops stormed the palace. They tore the great doors off their hinges and raided the treasury, packing the gold from the temple and carrying it off to their own land. And then they captured Manasseh, myself, and the other men who served in the temple.

Today, we are in chains, shuffling through the desert sands of Babylon. I know nothing of my fate. The heritage of my service to the living God is forever buried in Jerusalem, under the ashes of a burning palace. As we left the kingdom, our procession passed near Bethlehem, where my great-grandfather's brother's farm once stood. It had also been burnt with fire, the smoke rising into the sky.

Last night as our captors rested their horses, I tried to scrape the dust from my eyes with the chains that held my hands and feet. My mind drifted back many years to Isaiah's strange reaction to Hezekiah. I remembered the look in his eyes when he left Hezekiah's palace after telling him that he would be healed — and the look on his face as he stood watching our celebration. I suddenly realized that this day I was feeling what I saw in his eyes. Perhaps God's plan had been to end Hezekiah's life at the height of his kingdom, thus avoiding Manasseh's birth and the evil that he had brought to our kingdom.

Today I am still in service to the kings of Israel, as were my fathers before me. I have given my life to serve my king. In return, his evil heart has forever affected my life. His sin has changed my life forever, taking me far away from everything and everyone I knew and loved. Tonight as I search for restless sleep that will not come, I remember my father's words: "Righteousness exalts a nation, but sin is a disgrace to any people." How I wished that my king had heeded those words my father taught me as I served in the shadow of the throne.

Serving God with all your heart will affect your life and the lives of those around you. As you enter God's service, you take on a great responsibility to learn, grow, and remain faithful to Him so that He can work through you and your life. But at every step the Lord is present to assist you in your journey. Starting well will not prevent the later pressures of life, and you must constantly be on guard against subtle changes in your priorities. You can't mix your own will with God's and still experience all the blessings God has for your life.

Hezekiah's story is one of mixed motives, mixed blessings, and disastrous results. Hezekiah is one of the few kings noted in Isaiah's writings as a righteous leader. When he served God with all of his heart, God gave him success. But when he allowed other interests to influence his choices, he unleashed a Pandora's box into the lives of all those for whom he was responsible.

Hezekiah loved God. But somewhere along the path he forgot about Love's twin sister, Obedience. His life was marred by a solitary downfall: He regarded his own life to be more important than remaining in a loving, obedient relationship with his Father God.

Describe the relationship you see between love and obedience.

_____

_____

_____

_____

How was this relationship skewed in Hezekiah's life?

_____

_____

_____

How is this relationship manifested in your own life?

_____

_____

_____

_____

_____

_____

_____

And this leads us to the next principle in the process God uses to change hearts:

Principle Twelve: Love and obedience are forever linked as we mature in our relationship with God. Like twins in a womb, when it is time to be birthed, they must come into the world together, and together they will create a surrendered heart within us.

Day Three: At the Heart of the Issue, the Issue Is the Heart

As you live for God, twists and turns will arise that you never expected. The book of Proverbs says that a man may plan his ways, but it is the Lord who directs his steps (see Proverbs 16:9). It's the unexpected steps that can challenge your faith, resolve, and patience, but these challenges are what will expose your heart's deepest desires. Challenges are also often used by God to evaluate whether or not you are ready to receive His blessing. An unexpected challenge will expose your motives so that they become clear to you. God already knows what is in the deepest recesses of your heart. He knows what you will do in the face of a difficult decision. But He allows events — such as the dilemma presented to King Hezekiah — to expose to us what is in our hearts and further His process of molding us into His image.

This process plays out in every Christian's life, not just in the lives of kings and prophets. We are all called to take on the image of Christ. We are all asked to make decisions between what is popular, easy, expected, or right. We are all called to live in a manner that reflects God's heart to the world throughout our life. Hezekiah learned early the lessons of humility, honoring God, worship, and obedience to His Word. His choices brought success to the kingdom as he exalted God. But as his success grew, the very attention he received because of God's blessings actually became the next test. He grew comfortable. He enjoyed the fruits of God's blessing, but he grew to enjoy them more than the presence of God — and that was the beginning of his downfall.

Earlier we saw that the decisions Saul made in difficult times exposed his fears and insecurity. Hezekiah's decisions laid bare his greedy and selfish tendencies, his desire to have things his own way. When he talked himself out of obeying God's clear directive, he brought disaster to his kingdom, the people who followed him, and the people who loved him the most. The Amplified Version of the Bible contains this comment regarding Hezekiah's prayer for healing:

Good King Hezekiah's prayer life holds a mighty challenge and a clear and terrible warning for every believer. In his nation's darkest hour, he prayed and God performed a miracle, one He had foretold. It is a wonderful thing to have such power as that with God. In chapters 20 and 21 that power had become a terrible thing for Hezekiah who put himself on God's own ways and means committee. God clearly said, "Your time has come to die" (2 Kings 20:1). But Hezekiah's words and tears implied, "No, I want to live and have sons and do many things. I have the best of my years ahead of me."[1]

As you read further in chapter 20, you can note the terrible results of Hezekiah's decision — results that only God could have foreseen. Hezekiah's obedience would have prevented these events, but Hezekiah hijacked God's will, wrapped it in religious prayers, and slammed it headlong into God's good and perfect plan. The effects were disastrous as God's blessings slipped away. Eventually the consequences caused the entire kingdom to collapse as God's plan for peace and prosperity was buried in the rubble, replaced by immeasurable evil.

We have been given an awesome power and privilege as we enter into God's courts and make our requests known. God has promised that He will hear us, and when He hears, He has promised that He will answer. But will it be the answer that is best for us in the long run?

What do you do when you bring your prayer list to your heavenly Father? Do you demand your own desires or listen with a prepared heart, asking God what His desires are for you? Do you have a two-way conversation, listening for God's directives, or is your prayer time one-sided, with all of the talking being done on earth, and all of the responsibility for listening resting in heaven?

Today's written exercise is a practice in talking and then listening to God's reply. Throughout the last ten weeks you have written a number of prayer requests in this Bible study guide. There are prayers for your life, for events in your life, and for others. You have dug deeply into many areas of your faith and have put on paper the concerns that most deeply affect your life today.

Page back through some of your entries, and on the lines below, summarize one or two of the most important prayer requests you have made.

_____

_____

_____

_____

_____

_____

_____

_____

To finish today's work, spend time praying over these needs. Pause and listen to any reply that God may want to quietly speak to your heart. God often speaks with a quiet idea that comes to mind as you pray. Sometimes a verse of scripture will come to your mind that perfectly applies to your situation. But if the heavens are silent, that's okay too. God is often silent when He is working on some other area of your life.

When you are finished praying, thank God for the time you were able to spend in His presence, and record any thoughts you have below.

_____

_____

_____

_____

_____

_____

_____

_____

Day Four: Staying on Course

Hezekiah and Saul disappointed God because they allowed other interests and their personal weaknesses to interfere with their decision to serve Him wholeheartedly. Saul's decisions were based in the fears that held him captive from the very beginning of his reign. Hezekiah differs in that he started well but was pulled aside by cares which sprung up and choked the devotion out of his life.

Jesus told a similar story when His followers asked what the kingdom of God would be like.

Read Mark 4:1-20.

Jesus separated the seed which did not reach maturity or bear a harvest into three categories.

List the three categories, as well as the reason each did not reach full maturity.
1._____
2._____
3._____

To what does the "seed" and the "soil" refer in this passage?
_____
_____

Whom did Jesus say was the "fowl of the air" that snatched the Word away?
_____

To what is the seed sown on stony ground compared?
_____
_____

To what is the seed sown among thorns compared?

_____

_____

Some seeds fall on the hard ground of a person's heart, and the devil snatches it away before it can take root. Some seeds fall on shallow soil. Jesus said that when trials and afflictions come, these tender plants — that have started to grow — wither like a wildflower on the desert sand. This picture accurately portrays the reign of King Saul. The cares of his kingdom, his inner fears, and the pressure of his men's opinions of him were too great. He withered and spiritually lost his way.

The third group of unfruitful seeds fell in good soil and sent down strong roots. But these plants were challenged by other interests growing alongside of them. They fought the surrounding weeds for nourishment and water. Jesus called these weeds, _"worries of this life, the deceitfulness of wealth, and the desires for other things"_ (Mark 4:19).

Wild weeds are some of the thorniest plants. They are the "biker gangs" of the plant kingdom. Thorns and thistles can grow in the strangest of places, and short of harsh chemicals or a blow torch, there is often no way to kill them. Remaining for too long outside of the care and protection of God's kingdom has a way of producing a hardened attitude and a self-serving territorial nature. The weeds don't care whether the other plants around them grow or die; they only want to get what is "theirs." Personal selfish interests are like these weeds, and they will take over the garden of your heart if left unchecked.

Have you ever noticed that weeds have a way of returning when you are not paying attention? Every year my lawn is covered with dandelions, crab grass, and the like. If left on their own, they will take over the entire lawn in just a few short years. Since there is no way to prevent weeds, the only offense is a good defense that prepares the soil and combats the inevitable onslaught.

In the soil of our own hearts, we must continually prepare the ground for planting, breaking up the hardened soil, pulling up the weeds, and making sure all rocks are out of the pasture.

What did Jesus say about the seed that was sown on "good ground" (verse 20)?

_____

_____

_____

The garden you produce is up to you! How will you "prepare the soil"? In order to produce a bountiful harvest, what can you do to become ready for the "seed" of God's Word?

_____

_____

_____

What do you think? As you finish today's lesson, write your thoughts about the condition of your "heart's soil."

_____

_____

_____

_____

_____

Day Five: Voluntary Vulnerability

Hezekiah's life began well. The triumphs of his early reign set a standard for the kingdom and brought God's blessing back to the nation after decades of idolatrous kings. His "ground" was good ground, his heart prepared for a life of devotion and obedience.

Hezekiah knew God's plans for him. Isaiah's message was clear: God was calling him to his heavenly home. As he pleaded with God, "No, not Your way! I want my own way!" the surprising climax is that God said "okay," and allowed Hezekiah to have what he wanted. But Hezekiah's decision caused God's judgment to fall on the entire nation. Our all-powerful God can do anything. He doesn't have to listen to your arguments. He doesn't have to support your decisions. But in the same way that a loving parent will stand by and watch their children make poor decisions as they test their own wings, God also will allow you to choose foolishly in hopes that you will learn to listen to His Spirit the next time around.

Until the reign of Hezekiah's son Manasseh, whenever Israel's sinful behavior was mentioned in the Old Testament, God used King Ahab as His example. Ahab was a wicked king who had fought with the prophet Elijah 200 years earlier. God repeatedly warned Israel that they would be judged because of Ahab's sins. However, Manasseh's reign was so evil that God "updated" His notice warnings at that time, warning that it would be because of Manasseh that Israel would be destroyed. God judged Israel severely because of Manasseh's sins.

The prophet Jeremiah put it this way:

> Then the LORD said to me: "Even if Moses and Samuel were to stand before me, my heart would not go out to this people. Send them away from my presence! Let them go! And if they ask you, 'Where shall we go?' tell them, 'This is what the LORD says: "Those destined for death, to death; those for the sword, to the sword; those for starvation, to starvation; those for captivity, to captivity. I will send four kinds of destroyers against them," declares the LORD, "the sword to kill and the dogs to drag away and the birds of the air and the beasts of the earth to devour and

destroy. I will make them abhorrent to all the kingdoms of the earth because of what
Manasseh son of Hezekiah king of Judah did in Jerusalem." ' "

—Jeremiah 15:1-4

God was so angry that even if Moses or Samuel — two of the holiest prophets of Israel — were to personally pray for the nation, He would not listen. Under the influence of Manasseh, the country had fallen so far from following God that there was nothing that could convince God to withhold His hand of judgment. The crowning detail of this tragic epilogue is that Hezekiah could have prevented these events from taking place, but he chose himself instead of God — and that one decision set the tragedy in motion.

Our desires are often shrouded and difficult to discern. Your desire to have a better job, a bigger house, or a position of prominence at your job may be a part of God's plan — or it may not. While all of these are "good" things, God is more concerned about your character than the things or positions you have. It could be that He has some other higher plan for you. Here is an important lesson to learn: *God's primary purpose is to bring glory to Himself through you, and as a result of this, you will be blessed as well.* When you are part of God's work in the world and you see His Spirit touch others, then you are truly blessed. This blessing of ministering to others will also change you into the image of your heavenly Father as you take on His concerns and priorities, and you become willing to lay down your own life to see His kingdom come.

Think about the prayers and desires that have been at the top of your list, those things that you really want God to do in your life and the lives of others. Often the telltale sign of the motive behind a prayer is to see who will receive the glory if the prayer is answered. Of those things that are most often requested in your prayers, which demonstrate your desire for God's kingdom to come, and which demonstrate the seeking of your own glory? Write your thoughts below.

_____

_____

_____

_____

_____

_____

_____

A Community of Faith

Under the reign of Hezekiah's father, Ahaz, the land was filled with idols and pagan worship, and Ahaz himself even sacrificed some of his own children to the pagan idols. Into this environment Hezekiah was born. He may have even witnessed the sacrifice of his own brothers on pagan altars. Undoubtedly he watched the suffering of the country under his father's hand. But at the same time, he was being educated by Israel's priests and scribes. His life was shaped from an early age to look to the Lord Jehovah for blessing and guidance. Because Hezekiah was raised in the palace, he was raised in a community of faith, despite the fact that Ahaz was an idolatrous king. And when Hezekiah finally took the throne, his deepest desire was to see the blessing he had learned about from the priests return to his homeland. He had prepared good soil in his heart. As Hezekiah lived by God's principles, God brought more blessing and an increase in his power and the stature of his kingdom. With his prosperity came recognition from neighboring nations as well.

During this time, Hezekiah walked closely with God. He was surrounded by counselors, and during the initial times of testing, he drew close to Isaiah and spent time in the temple praying for God's deliverance. He made himself accountable and open to counselors and teachers. With their help, Hezekiah kept his eyes fixed on his Protector, Provider, and Shepherd. Through the community of faith that surrounded Hezekiah, he kept the fertile ground of his heart tilled and ready for God's kingdom to take root.

Jesus taught this same lifestyle by His example. For three years, He lived with His followers in a small community of faith. They traveled together and shared their lives. In a close setting such as this, one person's blind spots can be confronted by another and resolved. The weaknesses of one are built up by the strengths of another. They were accountable to each other, and they learned that the strength of the group was greater than the strength of the individuals alone. The strength of the one was greater because of the support and wisdom of the group behind him.

Staying on course — keeping the weeds from growing up in your life — is often a matter of staying connected to the church and remaining open and vulnerable to a small group of people who can give you loving support and advice.

In many churches, there has been a recent resurgence of small-group ministries. Across the country, many churches are realizing that when their numbers increase, the depth of ministry within the walls of the church building often decreases. Many small groups are growing as men and women seek to remain connected and allow God to prepare the "soil" in their hearts.

Do you have a small group of close Christian friends with whom you regularly meet? If so, do you meet often for Bible study, discussion, and prayer?

_____

_____

If you are a part of a small group, describe below what your group is like and how it has blessed your life. If you are not a part of a small group, describe the kind of group to which you would like to belong. How might you find such a group in which to participate?

_____

_____

_____

_____

_____

_____

_____

Note: If you are not already part of a group, the people participating in this twelve-week study with you are a terrific beginning for your own community of faith. The next time you meet to discuss this lesson, bring up the topic of small groups. If you are working through this book on your own, feel free to contact our office at the information provided at the back of the book. We will work to find a local church of your denomination or preference which has an active small-group ministry in your geo-graphical area.

There are three qualities which a small group will build into your life as brothers and sisters hold you accountable, and as God's mission becomes more and more your own. They are transparency, vulnerability, and humility. Let's take a look at each of them.

Transparency

How many people do you know who would describe the church as "just a bunch of hypocrites"? Many unbelievers would not darken the door of a church because they perceive that Christians are "phony" and "unreal." The reason for this is that many Christians are lacking *transparency* in their spiritual walk. When you are open and honest with others about yourself, your problems, and your faults, you develop transparency and others can see Christ working in you. Transparency will bridge the "phony Christian" gap.

Life isn't perfect, and neither are you. I don't know about your family, but my kids are some of the first to point out my faults! But because I am transparent with them, I don't hide my fears and struggles. Transparency allows others to see the real needs in your life. And then they — especially unbelievers — can see just how much Jesus is doing in you. It is not the "perfection" of a church body that will draw people in, but the level to which you can show them Jesus in a real world.

What comes to mind when you think of the term transparency as applied to a Christian's life?

_____

_____

_____

How can you become more transparent in your daily routines?

_____

_____

_____

Vulnerability

Opening your soul to others, being transparent with them, and allowing them to see that you are not perfect exposes you to the risk that others won't understand or that they will take advantage of you. It's much easier to maintain a plastic happy face, and when someone asks, "How are you doing today?" to toss back the perfunctory, "Fine. How are you?" How many times have you wanted someone to ask about your day and then really sit down and listen to your answer?

Most people are lucky to have even one or two trusted friends who know them well and are always ready to listen. But in today's fast-paced society, finding and maintaining these close connections is becoming increasingly difficult. The need, however, remains the same — the need for open, accountable relationships does not change because our culture has made these connections more difficult.

Choosing to be vulnerable exposes you to even more risk than transparency does. If you accept the risk of being open and vulnerable, you may find that others understand what you're going through, but reject you anyway. Don't be dismayed — God can use this rejection for a purpose! The greatest spiritual growth in Joseph and David's lives came about as a result of the confusion and hurt they felt when those they trusted the most betrayed them. However, not everyone responds to such events like Joseph and David did. These offenses can easily sprout roots of unforgiveness, which can quickly grow up into a bitter attitude. While Joseph and David were able to trust in God to see them through, many believers become sidelined by anger, unforgiveness, and bitterness which gradually poison every relationship in their lives.

The church should be a place where vulnerability without rejection is encouraged and practiced. Within a small community of faith — such as a small group setting — you should be loved and accepted for who you are, while at the same time encouraged to grow in Christ. These relationships can become a keel under your little boat, making it possible to maintain a straight course even in strong crosswinds and adverse tides.

When you think of an accountable community of faith, what ideas come to mind? It may be that the thought of being so "tight" with such a group of people is threatening to you. The American culture has grown increasingly hostile over the past decades. It has become commonplace to reject anyone or anything that doesn't "fit the mold," but rejection and misunderstanding have a way of building up walls around the hearts of people as they seek to protect themselves from further hurt. The most tragic effect of a heart that hardens itself against the outside world is that it also becomes hardened to God's Spirit. It is impossible to love God and hate people. It is equally impossible to be open to God and remain closed to the needs and desires of others.

In a truly loving small community of faith, the walls can come down. Genuine love creates a trusting environment in which God is present in His people, and through the love of others, people can experience God's own love and acceptance that will change their hearts.

Do you find it easy or difficult to be vulnerable with others?

_____

_____

Have you ever experienced God's love through the love and acceptance of a friend or a group of people with whom you were vulnerable? Explain.

_____

_____

_____

_____

How could you become more vulnerable in your daily life?

_____

_____

_____

Humility

Humility is one of those words that are hard to define. We can all recognize when someone is being humble — and when they are not! But it is not enough to define a humble person as someone who is not excessively proud. The color "black" cannot be defined simply as the absence of white, and "clean" clothes aren't just those clothes possessing the absence of dirt!

When Jesus described a humble heart, He encouraged His listeners to learn from His own lifestyle. Jesus said, "Take my yoke upon you and learn of Me. I am gentle and humble of heart. If you follow My example, you will find rest for your soul" (see Matthew 11:28-29).

When Jesus was pressured by the crowd, He stayed true to His Father's purposes. When He was pressured by the demands of a busy schedule, He maintained His habit of prayer. Jesus made time to take children onto His lap and bless them. He also spoke His mind with love and compassion to saints and sinners alike; He was not afraid of their opinion of Him or whether or not they would accept His message.

If Jesus had been full of pride, He would have taken all of the problems back onto Himself. A lack of humility would have caused Jesus to focus on His own importance, more than the needs of others. But Jesus did not do that. And He was more than just "not proud" — He actively and humbly set aside His own agenda and obeyed His Father. Jesus remained true to His Father's plan and left the results in the hands of the One who was big enough to worry about it.

How do you see humility exhibited in the life of Jesus?

_____

_____

_____

In what ways can you exercise more humility in your own life?

_____

_____

_____

Transparency, vulnerability, and humility are refreshing rest stops along the road to a softened, pure heart. You were meant for community, to give and receive love, because you have been created in the image and likeness of God, the greatest Love-Giver of all!

Father God,

Allowing You to create a tender heart within me is a difficult process. Help me to become more transparent, vulnerable, and humble with those You have placed in my life. It would be so much easier to stay behind my protective barriers, but You sent Your Son to show me how to live. Jesus deliberately left the security of heaven and took enormous risks in order to demonstrate to us what an abundant life looked like. Jesus, You were rejected and misunderstood. You were loved by some and hated by others. You have shown us how to "get real" by giving Yourself to others and allowing the Father to work out the consequences. Jesus, I want to be more like You. Allow me to be a demonstration of Your love in my world. Amen.

Week Eleven: Summary

They devoted themselves to the apostles' teaching and to the fellowship, to the breaking of bread and to prayer. Everyone was filled with awe, and many wonders and miraculous signs were done by the apostles. All the believers were together and had everything in common. Selling their possessions and goods, they gave to anyone as he had need. Every day they continued to meet together in the temple courts. They broke bread in their homes and ate together with glad and sincere hearts, praising God and enjoying the favor of all the people. And the Lord added to their number daily those who were being saved.

—Acts 2:42-47

All the believers were one in heart and mind. No one claimed that any of his possessions was his own, but they shared everything they had. With great power the apostles continued to testify to the resurrection of the Lord Jesus, and much grace was upon them all.

—Acts 4:32-33

This lesson has introduced you to new ideas about King Hezekiah and the ways in which God wanted to work in his life. If there is one insight or idea that summarizes what you have learned this week, write it on the lines below.

_____

_____

_____

_____

_____

_____

_____

_____

Hezekiah

Seeking God's Glory, or Your Own?

For we do not have a high priest who is unable to sympathize with our weaknesses.... Let us then approach the throne of grace with confidence, so that we may receive mercy and find grace to help us in our time of need.

—Hebrews 4:15-16

Day One: Take a Look at God's Word

If there is one person in the kingdom who bore the responsibility of keeping the king in line with God's will — besides the king himself — that person was the prophet. Prophets came to the table with a black-and-white view of life. Right was right, wrong was wrong, and in the prophets' minds, there were few reasons for blurring the line between the two. The Old Testament prophets were fiery characters who often did strange things in order to grab the people's attention. Only part of the time did prophets declare future events. Their primary purpose was to impress on the people the gravity of the situation when idolatry or religious ritual had displaced a pure-hearted zeal for the living God. Prophets concerned themselves with the hearts of the people. Whether they declared impending doom or the promise of God's blessing, their matter-of-fact approach expressed a true heart of God's jealousy for His people.

By the time Isaiah became Hezekiah's counsel, he had already preached the message of repentance throughout Israel for over fifty years. Isaiah's purpose with regard to Hezekiah was to focus the king on maintaining a pure heart before the King of all kings. The record given in Isaiah 36-39 is much more personal than that of the Israelite scribe who wrote the book of 2 Kings. As you read these chapters, look closely at the personal interaction between Isaiah, Hezekiah, and the messages from God. Also pay attention to the content of Hezekiah's prayers recorded in chapter 38. You will see much of Hezekiah's heart exposed in these prayers.

As you read through each chapter, determine what interaction is taking place between God, Isaiah, and Hezekiah. Record your thoughts in the lines below.

Isaiah 36

_____

_____

_____

_____

_____

_____

Isaiah 37

_____

_____

_____

_____

_____

_____

Isaiah 38

_____

_____

_____

_____

_____

_____

Isaiah 39

_____

_____

_____

_____

_____

_____

Day Two: Prayer: The Internal Gauge of Your Heart

Looking back at the repercussions of Hezekiah's decisions, we can see the seriousness of demanding our own way. After enjoying God's benefits and blessing on the nation as a whole, Hezekiah assumed that God was blessing him *for the blessings' sake.* Hezekiah wanted the total focus of God's divine attention on himself. God's ultimate will was not the focus of his prayers and even though God answered them, the results were disastrous. Hezekiah took the foolish step from Point A, in which he enjoyed the blessings of God's favor, to Point B, in which he assumed that God's purpose is always to bless.

Jesus was tempted by Satan with a similar assumption in the desert. Satan led Jesus to the highest point of a tall building and suggested that He throw Himself down. Surely God would catch Him! How could the Father God allow anything "bad" to happen to His only Son? Satan even used scripture to support his claim. (See Matthew 4:5-7.) Unfortunately, "it must be that this is what God wants…" are the infamous last words of many biblical heroes who forgot about serving God on their way to serve themselves.

So, how can we tell when we are making the same presumptuous leap when we bring our requests before God? In other words, how can we judge our own motives?

How do you usually judge the motives of your own heart?

_____

_____

_____

_____

_____

_____

The books of Psalms and Proverbs zero in on a believer's heart more than any other topic. There are over two hundred references to a "pure heart," a "wise heart," and serving God "with all your heart" in these two books alone. In addition, the largest single topic of the prophetic books was also serving or returning to the Lord with all your heart. The prophets wove word pictures about Israel's future and occasionally declared oracles about future events, but the prophets' message, which fills a quarter of the Old Testament, was one of the heart. Your heart and motives are so important to the Lord, that evaluating them and maintaining their purity are made a top priority in His Book!

Your prayers are an internal thermometer that gauges the temperature of your devotion. A heart that is truly on fire for God will focus on God's kingdom and glory. There is no cost that seems too high to pay for a person who is serving God with single-hearted devotion. A slightly warm heart that struggles with divided interests will reveal telltale signs of this in the content of its prayers. A lukewarm interest in God will become painfully evident by the words you speak and the desires to which you cling. (See Matthew 12:34-35.) But a cold heart is not likely to have any prayer life at all. Regardless of any of your other "spiritual" habits, if your prayer life has grown cold, so has the fervor of your heart.

The events we considered last week did not offer much insight into Hezekiah's devotion. He made a fatal mistake at the end of his reign, but there is little scriptural evidence that identifies why he made the choice he did. But because this story is recorded in two places in Scripture — in 2 Chronicles and in the book of Isaiah — we can dig deeper. Isaiah devotes an entire chapter to Hezekiah's illness and his personal interaction with the king. Let's consider Hezekiah's prayer for healing and his psalm of rejoicing when his prayer was answered.

Read Isaiah 38:9-21.

What are your initial thoughts about Hezekiah's prayers?

_____

_____

_____

_____

_____

As you read through this prayer, the words _I, me,_ and _mine_ are used in almost every line. There is something strangely missing in the prayers that insist on your own rights from God. What's missing is devotion and humility. Hezekiah's heart had lost the reverence and fear of God that is necessary to hear God and accept God's decisions in his life.

When you pray, do you seek your own desires or do you pray, God, *Your kingdom come. Your will be done in my life on earth, as it is done in heaven?* Record your thoughts below.

_____

_____

_____

_____

_____

It's been said that the true measure of your heart is not what you do in public, but what you desire when you are alone. Let's make a comparison to a prayer made by David, the "man after God's own heart." In 1 Chronicles 17, King Saul had died, and David was finally established in his kingdom, ruling over both northern and southern tribes. He was the king and was recognized as such by all of Israel. After he ascended to the throne, David greatly desired to build a temple for the Lord. For the more than five hundred years that Israel had dwelt in the Promised Land, the Ark of the Covenant remained in a tent. But as his ordeal in the desert ended, David wanted to build a monument to the God who had protected him through the darkest time of his life.

We know from history that David did not build the temple. This was a task that God gave to David's son Solomon — even though it was the deepest desire of David's heart. In 1 Chronicles 17 David shared his desire with the prophet Nathan, asking Nathan to pray about his role in such a project. Nathan returned the next day with this reply: "No, you're not going to be the one to build the temple. You have been a man of war. Your son will do what you want to do." Like Hezekiah, the deep desire of his heart was not in God's will. But David's desire wasn't selfish — he wanted to honor his God as the nation now honored him. Such was the response of a heart that had been broken and then rebuilt.

In contrast to Hezekiah, David's response to God's answer arose from a heart that trusted God and wanted to give Him his personal best.

Read David's prayer in 1 Chronicles 17.
How does the focus of David's prayer differ from that of Hezekiah's?

_____

_____

_____

_____

There is a striking contrast between this prayer and Hezekiah's prayer three hundred years later. Words that were so prominent in Hezekiah's prayer are glaringly absent from David's, words such as *I, I have, I wish, and I want. Instead, David said:*

- *"You, O Lord are great."*
- *"You have blessed me, Your servant."*
- *"You have reached down and made a people to Yourself."*
- *"You have lifted up my house."*
- *"You have made a promise to me."*

David had not learned from success but from trial. David had learned on the back side of the desert to trust God's redemptive hand in all circumstances. Neither people's praise nor the power of his throne was able to corrupt his devotion because he sought after the desires of his God. No one can deny that David received blessings larger than his life could hold, but David did not seek the blessings. David sought God.

On a scale of 1 to 10, with 1 being a cold, unresponsive heart and 10 being a heart on fire for God, rate your devotion.

_____

How do you see yourself in terms of listening to, responding to, and obeying the living God?

_____

_____

What issue in your life might be standing in the way of your becoming more closely devoted to the Father, both in heart and in action? Write below the first thing that comes to your mind.

_____

_____

_____

What can you do to change the situation?

_____

_____

_____

_____

_____

Day Three: A Heart Reveals Itself by Remaining Faithful

There was a flaw in both David and Hezekiah's lives — and it is one that is present in us all. That fatal flaw is, at its root, selfishness.

Hezekiah began his reign as a man devoted to God. He was remembered as a man likened to his ancestor David. He tore down the idols, restored the temple, rebuilt the gates, and created marvelous architectural works around Jerusalem. He restored the people's sense of pride and honor in themselves and their God. And in response, God prospered him. Unfortunately, as his prosperity grew, so did Hezekiah's desire to continue in the prosperity.

David's life shared this same blemish. The one black mark on David's exemplary life is his adulterous affair with Bathsheba and the actions he took following it. When Bathsheba discovered she was pregnant, David arranged her husband's murder. In response, God exacted immediate judgment, and the child of their union became ill and promptly died.

This entire episode in David's life is recorded in 2 Samuel 11, and it is telling to see that all of the heartache and tragedy began with just these few simple words.

Read 2 Samuel 11:1.
Now, write the final phrase of the verse in the space below.

Why would the phrase, "David tarried in Jerusalem," be significant? In the spring of each year, kings went out to war in order to protect their citizens from hungry, rival neighbors. David had learned during his time in the wilderness that the winter's barrenness created hungry Bedouins. It was no surprise to David that when spring arrived, hostile tribes would swoop down on the outlying Israelite villages and steal supplies, food, and women for themselves. As a shepherd watches over his flock, every spring David would mount a campaign to protect his people.

What was different about this particular year?

_____

_____

_____

_____

_____

This year, David remained home, relaxing in his success. Joab was the trusted general and his faithful friend. He had served at David's side for over three decades, and David decided to delegate this responsibility to his key general. This was David's first, and possibly greatest, mistake. Had David been with his troops where he belonged, he would not have been lying around on the roof of his palace in the middle of the day, ogling his neighbor's wife.

Principle Thirteen: In becoming men or women through whom God can work, we must serve God with all our heart. This means remaining faithful to what God has given us to do. God calls us to faithfulness in our inner, vertical relationship to Him, and in our outer, horizontal relationships with others.

There may be times when you long for change, but God honors faithfulness. You may long for a change of pace, but the reality of spiritual discipline is that it is sometimes hard work! God will use this yoke of responsibility to guide your heart toward the direction of further devotion to Him — and to keep you safe from consequences that could change the rest of your life.

One afternoon in our small group, we were discussing the topic of temptation and how to avoid it, and a friend relayed a situation he continually faced. Jim (his name has been changed) is a college professor, and is frequently approached by students for extra-credit work to rescue a failing grade. At times he is approached by attractive female coeds who, in the privacy of his office, will volunteer to do "anything" to raise their grades. Jim's response is one from which both David and Hezekiah could have learned a great deal. Before the atmosphere in the room gets any steamier, Jim opens his office door. He does not allow the conversation to head down that slippery slope. And through accountability to the others in his office, Jim keeps his mind, his heart — and his actions — pure.

Have you ever been in a situation in which opportunity fertilized the ground, allowing temptation and carnal desires to sprout?

_____

_____

_____

These can be opportunities to either build your faith or surrender to selfishness. Which was the case in your situation?

_____

_____

_____

_____

Is there currently a situation in your life in which it is difficult for you to maintain your purity? Men and women have different temptations, and there are situations that create unique struggles for each gender. Honestly review your desires and hold them up to God's desires for you. Is there a specific area that should have a "Do Not Enter" sign posted on the door?

_____

_____

_____

_____

_____

_____

What can you do to strengthen your resolve to follow God's will in your life? Saul fell because he didn't obey God with his whole heart. Hezekiah was led away from devotion by his prosperity and desire to have his own way.

In the light of the weaknesses you listed above, what specific actions can you take to strengthen your will and make God the object of highest devotion in your heart?

_____

_____

_____

_____

The final epitaph for Hezekiah's life is given in 2 Chronicles 32. Written toward the end of his reign, the scribes recorded this commemoration:

It was Hezekiah who blocked the upper outlet of the Gihon spring and channeled the water down to the west side of the City of David. He succeeded in everything he undertook. But when envoys were sent by the rulers of Babylon to ask him about the miraculous sign that had occurred in the land {Hezekiah's healing from his deadly illness}, God left him to test him and to know everything that was in his heart.

—Verses 30-31

When Hezekiah prayed, God saw in his prayer the selfishness that Hezekiah himself could not see. And after granting his request, God waited to see who would receive the glory and who would be thanked. True to his heart, Hezekiah took the credit and seemed to forget about God, basking in the praise and admiration of his neighbors. When the princes of Babylon heard that his health had been miraculously restored, they visited to pay homage to the king. In response, the proud king showed them all the treasures in his kingdom and the splendor of the temple. He assumed personal ownership of and responsibility for everything God had given him, and so set the stage for the end of his kingdom.

Record your final thoughts about Hezekiah's life on the lines below, as well as any application that stands out to you from this lesson.

_____

_____

_____

_____

_____

_____

_____

Day Four: A Heart Reveals Itself by What It Does

We have now completed our specific study on the lives of David, Joseph, Saul, and Hezekiah. Today we are going to examine scripture verses that will further reinforce the lessons you've learned during the past twelve weeks. Many of these verses will be familiar to you, but in light of this study, they may have new meaning for you. Unless you are an avid Bible student, other verses may be completely new to you. But as you read each verse, regardless of how familiar it is to you, pause to consider how the living God may want to apply it in your life.

Each word in the Bible was written for you. God crafted this love letter just for you, so that you can know Him more completely and experience the fullness of life He wants to provide for you. The path to a life of true blessing and fulfillment is illuminated by God's Word. Psalm 119:105 says that God's Word is a lamp to your feet and a light to your path. By reading the Bible, you can begin to walk a path that will bring you closer to God and cause you to be more devoted to His heart.

Read each of the verses below, and write out the main theme of each. **What does each have to say about your devotion to God and your becoming a person after His own heart?**

Proverbs 2:2-5

_____

_____

Proverbs 3:5-6

_____

_____

Proverbs 4:20-23

_____

_____

Proverbs 14:14

_____

_____

Proverbs 19:3

_____

_____

Isaiah 29:13

_____

_____

Jeremiah 29:11-13

_____

_____

Joel 2:12-13

_____

_____

God's Word has the power to initiate change in your life! When Jesus was tempted by the devil, He used scripture to defeat the enemy and remain fixed on the will of the Father. In your own life, memorizing God's Word can give you the inner strength you need to overcome temptation and better understand the plan of God for you. Pick out one passage from those you have just read and make a commitment to memorize it over the next week. This will strengthen your faith and release God's power in your life.

Write the complete text of the verse you select below.

_____

_____

_____

_____

Because Day 5 this week is the last day of our study together, we will take that opportunity to review the last twelve weeks and the lessons we have learned. To allow for that time, the summary for week twelve follows today's lesson.

Week Twelve: Summary

For this reason I kneel before the Father, from whom his whole family in heaven and on earth derives its name. I pray that out of his glorious riches he may strengthen you with power through his Spirit in your inner being, so that Christ may dwell in your hearts through faith. And I pray that you, being rooted and established in love, may have power, together with all the saints, to grasp how wide and long and high and deep is the love of Christ, and to know this love that surpasses knowledge — that you may be filled to the measure of all the fullness of God. Now to him who is able to do immeasurably more than all we ask or imagine, according to his power that is at work within us, to him be glory in the church and in Christ Jesus throughout all generations, for ever and ever! Amen.

—Ephesians 3:14-21

This lesson has introduced you to new ideas about King Hezekiah and the ways in which God wanted to work in his life. If there is one insight or idea that summarizes what you have learned this week, write it on the lines below.

_____

_____

_____

_____

_____

_____

_____

_____

Day Five: The Signs of a Changed Heart

As we have seen in our journey into the lives of these four rulers, God looks at the heart of a person before He considers the outward appearance. God is much more concerned with what is going on in your heart than anything else, because eventually what is in your heart will appear on the surface of your life. You can learn new habits like you can put on new clothes. You can put a new coat of paint on a decaying old building. But when God moves in, He wants nothing less than a totally revived heart — from the inside out — a heart that is solely focused on bringing glory and honor to Him.

On the final page of each week of lessons, you were asked to write a single insight or idea that had made an impact on you during your study. By doing so, you have slowly drafted a personal account of God's work in your life. You may not have noticed, but there is very likely a theme that runs through your entries and focuses on one or two issues that God has put on your heart right now.

One purpose of this Bible study was to highlight lessons from these rulers' lives to show how God can create a tender heart in your life. The second — and greater — purpose is to allow a personal encounter between yourself and the living God to take place.

When you meet God face to face, you will be forever transformed. David met God through His provision in the wilderness, and it forever changed him into a man after God's own heart. Joseph met God in the dreams of his youth, and when those dreams were fulfilled, an arrogant brat was transformed into the humble leader of the most powerful kingdom on earth. Had Saul and Hezekiah remained in God's prep school, there is no telling what great things He would have done through their lives.

God also wants to do great things through you! His plan begins when you enter His presence and allow Him to personally change you. Sounds exciting, doesn't it? To be a servant of the powerful, wonderful, loving Creator of the universe…what could be a higher calling?

The final assignment in our study is to sketch out what God is using to work in your life. Turn back to the last page of each week's lessons, and write on the lines below the primary idea you learned each week. You may already know what God is doing in your life, and this exercise will be an encouraging confirmation of His work in your heart. You may be in a desert, looking for God's fingerprint in the sand. This review will begin to identify what treasures God is teaching you. If you have drifted from His purpose and the fire in your heart has dwindled to a pile of cooling embers, this exercise will be a significant step in restoring your heart to the devotion it once had for the living God.

David
Week 1: Beginning a personal relationship with God

_____

_____

Week 2: Constructing character through faithful friends and unexpected events

_____

_____

Week 3: Making choices based on God's guidance

_____

_____

Week 4: Experiencing the everyday blast furnace of life

_____

_____

Joseph
Week 5: Strengthening your inner desire for godliness

_____

_____

Week 6: Making decisions in the desert of quiet, faithful service

_____

_____

Week 7: Holding onto God's promises through turbulent times

_____

_____

Week 8: Leading others in heart transformation

_____

_____

Saul

Week 9: Waiting on God, or performing for man's approval

_____

_____

Week 10: Descending slowly into compromise

_____

_____

Hezekiah

Week 11: Nursing divided interests

_____

_____

Week 12: Seeking God's glory, or your own

_____

_____

After considering the lessons you have learned each week, can you see a dominant theme emerging throughout the entire study? Are you just beginning your faith walk in God's kingdom? Are you in the desert of God's preparation? Are you "stuck" in your faith because difficult events caught you off guard?

In whatever stage of the Christian life you are walking, choose one central theme you have learned from this study, and write it on the lines below.

_____

_____

_____

_____

Now let's consider each principle we have looked at in the process of becoming a person "after God's own heart."

As you read through each principle, determine which have been implemented into your life and which you still need to work on. Place a checkmark beside the principles on which you still need to focus, and then, in the lines following, explain how you might begin to implement that principle into your life.

Principle One: We meet God, begin a personal relationship with Him, and receive a personal revelation of His love for us.

_____

_____

_____

_____

Principle Two: God provides the opportunity for a period of initial peace, victory, or success, but then He shapes your life through circumstances, events, or other people. Through true friends, false alliances, and suffering injustice or other hardships, He sculpts Christ-like character into our selfish hearts. This process can be painful, but the final result is that we become more like Jesus.

_____

_____

_____

_____

Principle Three: God's loving tests continue until we come to a place of utter dependence on Him. We learn to look to Him and behave in ways consistent with God's character, regardless of whatever injustice, trial, or opportunity for temporary personal gain comes our way.

_____

_____

_____

_____

Principle Four: Adolescent leaders, regardless of their age, are tested before they are released. The choices they make define and refine their godly character in the blast furnace of life.

_____

_____

_____

_____

Principle Five: We find the courage and personal strength to remain faithful to our beliefs because of positive mentoring relationships in our life. As a child or as an adult, mentoring relationships are necessary to change our heart and mold our character into a vessel that God can use.

_____

_____

_____

_____

Principle Six: God will often use the desert of quiet faithful service or the prison of injustice, to permanently transform our self-confidence into Christ-confidence. It is only when control is out of our own hands and we are thrust blindly into God's arms that He is free to teach us that He can be completely relied upon.

_____

_____

_____

_____

Principle Seven: Only after we pass tests in the pit of pride, the plateaus of faithful service, and the prison of injustice, and we demonstrate proof of our character through our decisions, are we ready to receive God's promises. If we stray from this character-smelting process, it is possible to delay or completely abort the great revelations of God's character and faithfulness that He has planned to reveal through us.

_____

_____

_____

_____

Principle Eight: After learning the lessons of mercy and justice, we may still see difficulty in the lives of those we love, as God works to build the same character in their lives as He built in ours.

_____

_____

_____

_____

Principle Nine: Personal obedience to God is a cornerstone of our love relationship with Him. Partial obedience, delayed obedience, or altering God's requests to fit our own desires or lifestyle, is disobedience, and is irrefutable proof of a divided heart.

_____

_____

_____

_____

Principle Ten: The weaknesses in our character can lie hidden at first, but they will come to light in the decisions that we make. Mixed motives will eventually betray the self-centered nature of our choices and priorities.

_____

_____

_____

_____

Principle Eleven: Tension, struggle, and conflict will always be a part of life. Our faith rises to new heights by overcoming these challenges.

_____

_____

_____

_____

Principle Twelve: Love and obedience are forever linked as we mature in our relationship with God. Like twins in a womb, when it is time to be birthed, they must come into the world together, and together they will create a surrendered heart within us.

_____

_____

_____

_____

Principle Thirteen: In becoming a person through whom God can work, we must serve God with all our heart. This means remaining faithful to what God has given us to do. God calls us to faithfulness in our inner, vertical relationship to Him, and in our outer, horizontal relationships with others.

_____

_____

_____

_____

God is at work in your life right now! He wants you to know that He is at work, and He wants you to trust Him and allow Him into your life more completely. Now that you have identified the message that God has revealed to you from these pages, finish this Bible study with a prayer of consecration. Give the Lord your whole heart, mind, soul, and strength. Allow God to rule and reign in your heart, just like the rulers we have studied ruled from their thrones. No one questioned their authority or argued with their requests. When you allow Jesus Christ to be Lord of all, the exceeding great Treasure of your life, you too will become a person after God's own heart.

My Prayer of Consecration:

_____

_____

_____

_____

_____

_____

_____

_____

Notes

Introduction

[1]Charles Spurgeon, *God Promises You* (New Kensington, PA: Whitaker, 1995), 167-168.

Week 11

[1] *The Amplified Bible* (Grand Rapids: Zondervan Bible Publishers, 1987), 450.

WE WANT TO KNOW WHAT YOU THINK ABOUT THIS STUDY!

Please share your comments about this study by posting your review on our website. From the menu bar at the top of the Hensley Publishing home page, select **Our Products**. On the Products page, scroll down the page until you see the cover of the Bible study. Choose the study by clicking on the cover image. On the next screen, select **Write a Review** in the right column. Write your review and click on **Submit**.

You can see our complete line of Bible studies, post a review, or order online and save at:

www.hensleypublishing.com

HENSLEY
PUBLISHING

6116 E 32nd St.
Tulsa, OK 74135

Toll Free Ordering: 800.288.8520
Fax: 918.664.8562
Phone: 918.664.8520

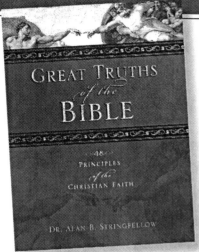
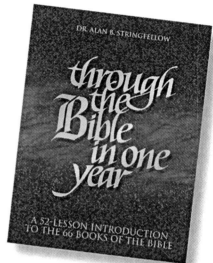
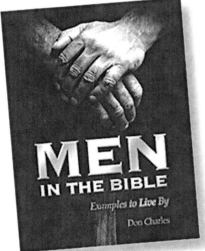

Printed in the United States
96128LV00002B/1-44/A